Turmeric

Herb of the Year™ 2026

International Herb Association

Compiled and edited by Kathleen Connole

IHA Herb of the Year™

Each year the International Herb Association chooses an **Herb of the Year™** to highlight. The Horticulture Committee evaluates possible choices based on their being outstanding in at least two of the three major categories: culinary, medicinal, and ornamental. Herbal organizations around the world work together with us to educate the public throughout the year.

Herb of the Year™ books are published annually by the

International Herb Association
P.O. Box 5667 Jacksonville, Florida 32247-5667
www.iherb.org

This book is intended as an informational guide. The remedies, approaches, and techniques described herein are meant to supplement and not to be a substitute for professional medical care or treatment; please consult your health care provider.

The International Herb Association is a professional trade organization providing education, service, and development for members engaged in all aspects of the herbal industry.

ISBN: 979-8-9878959-6-2

Uniting Herb Professionals for Growth
Through Promotion and Education

The International Herb Association has some of the most dedicated volunteers who keep the organization afloat, giving their time and talents to ensure that IHA continues to share herbal knowledge and connect those in the profession of herbs. We are deeply indebted to the IHA Board of Directors and the IHA Foundation members. Thanks for all that you do and for caring enough to move us forward!

Acknowledgments

For this, my 5th year as the Editor of Herb of the Year, we are studying perhaps one of the most powerful yet very ancient herbs, turmeric. The job of being editor has been very challenging—so much to learn about the process (more every time!)—and rewarding, to work with so many knowledgeable individuals who are passionate about herbs.

Turmeric is a tropical plant, but our growers and gardeners have demonstrated that one does not have to live in the tropics to grow this incredible plant. Susan Belsinger and Tina Marie Wilcox have grown turmeric and its relative ginger for years in containers; they provide instructions on how to overwinter it in colder climates, propagation, and how to keep its foliage from burning up in the hot Arkansas summer. Lucie and Matt Day show us how well this plant can do, given their expert care, favorable climate, superb soil, and a high tunnel greenhouse to extend the season—necessary for this plant to reach its full potential—amazing! Rosemary Davis gives a detailed overview of the natural history of turmeric as it traveled the world and became integrated into many cultures for dye, food, and medicine. Jane Stevens shares her experiences and success growing turmeric in containers and explains the differences between planting and harvesting in one season, versus wintering over to allow two seasons of growth. Janice Cox's very interesting craft of making sun prints could be a fun and educational project to look forward to doing with friends and children. Gert Coleman shares some beautiful and inspiring examples of customs observing turmeric's spiritual significance that began in ancient times and continue to this day.

The recipes presented are some of the most varied yet, providing delicious ideas for how we can incorporate this powerhouse herb into our daily diets—lovely spice mixes, condiments, beverages, snacks, sides and main dishes, and desserts. Thanks to our culinary artists Susan Belsinger, Pat Crocker, Rosemary Davis, Karen England, and Carol Little. Skye Suter grew up enjoying the ethnic Indian recipes and shares beautiful recipes from her childhood. Chuck Voigt's "Concrete Pickles" are surely one of a kind.

Turmeric really has its greatest impact as a very powerful medicinal herb. Susan Belsinger shares her long history with Golden Milk, and a recipe for bitters—with information about the unusual and extremely bitter blue turmeric. Recipes from Janice Cox are for lovely external applications, to soothe and heal skin. Carol Little gives us her simple folk method to make turmeric tincture. Daniel Gagnon and Dorene Petersen provide us with the most up-to-date information on the incredible healing properties of turmeric, with in-depth examination of the medicinal constituents. Dorene has included recipes for her healing formulations. Marge Powell gives us a pictorial demonstration on how she incorporates turmeric into both her liquid and bar soap recipes.

We greatly appreciate the photographs contributed by Susan Belsinger, Janice Cox, Pat Crocker, Lucie Day, Karen England, Pat Kenny, Alicia Mann, Helen Lowe Metzman, Dorene Petersen, Douglas Reingold, Jane Hawley Stevens and Chuck Voigt. They make the book much more colorful and interesting!

Thanks to our artists Pat Kenny, Gail Miller and Skye Suter; Pat also shared her photos of her turmeric harvesting project and her glorious turmeric porch plant.

Susan Belsinger composed the lovely haikus and gave us her vision of the beautiful cover design.

We could not put together such a beautiful, professional book without our talented graphic designer, Heather Cohen. Heather is very helpful and patient, while making sure that we keep the process moving along, to get the book ready to print as soon as possible.

I wish to express my deepest gratitude, words are not enough, to our proofreaders and editorial consultants, Susan Belsinger, Gert Coleman, and Karen Kalergis.

My words in closing *Chamomile Herb of the Year 2025* still apply, and so I will say, it is sometimes a challenge for my family members to understand the obsessive behavior that occurs during the production of these books. I am very grateful for their tolerance, encouragement, and support, without which it would not be possible.

~ Kathleen Connole

Table of Contents

Turmeric for Health & Beauty

Pronouncing Turmeric

Gert Coleman

While we celebrate Turmeric as the 2026 Herb of the Year, we should consider how best to pronounce it.

The standard, dictionary-preferred pronunciation is TERM – er – ick. Both R sounds are enunciated.

However, many folks pronounce it as TOOM-er-ick. I have heard herbal experts use both pronunciations in the same lecture. Which is correct?

Once considered the substandard pronunciation, this variant has become quite common in the United States. When mispronounced words enter common usage, their endurance brings acceptance. While this pronunciation bothers some of us, with its inadvertent enunciation of tumor, dictionaries now authorize the American variant TOOM-er-ick as a second standard pronunciation.

Maybe turmeric's superstar status as a healthful supplement, with its possible ability to prevent cancers, is pushing our thoughts in that direction.

So, while you say TOOM-er-ick, I say TERM – er – ick. We are both correct.

Shaded turmeric and ginger growing in the Herb of the Year bed at the Ozark Folk Center State Park, Mountain View, Arkansas. *Susan Belsinger*

Knowing
&
Growing
Turmeric

Trimmed and cured rhizomes are planted, with growth buds facing up, in 4 1/2-inch pots in flats for sprouting in Harbinger Farm's greenhouse. *Lucie Day*

Our Experience Cultivating & Harvesting Turmeric

Tina Marie Wilcox & Susan Belsinger

Turmeric (*Curcuma longa*) is a member of the Zingiberaceae family and an exotic tropical herb that we love to grow and use; turmeric and ginger have very similar growing and harvesting conditions. Though we refer to the underground parts as "roots"—and they do have botanical roots—the parts we desire to consume are really underground stems, called a rhizome, which have the ability to grow stems, leaves, and flowers.

Growing basics

- Subtropical or tropical plants must be brought indoors for winter before temperatures drop below 50°F.
- Hardiness zones 7 to 11; foliage will die back in winter
- Full sun to part shade
- Prefers adequate moisture during the growing season, though soil must be well-drained
- Sandy-loam, neutral to alkaline soil; pH 5.5 to 6.5
- Turmeric's growing season is 10 months. Fingers can be dug for fresh use anytime.

Cultivation and propagation

Turmeric has clusters or "hands" that are rhizomorphous. These are thickened, modified underground stems, which produce roots below and shoots aboveground. Home gardeners can purchase turmeric "seed" online, from garden catalogs, or may occasionally find nursery-grown plants. Tissue cultured seed is preferred by many because it is disease free.

Fresh turmeric sold in produce markets is the fastest, though not the safest, propagation stock to obtain. The danger is that field grown rhizomes can be infected with microscopic nematodes or fungal diseases including bacterial wilt, *Fusarium*, *Pythium*, and *Rhizoctonia*. Before learning about the availability of seed turmeric, Tina started her first plants from the produce market and had success. If you decide to use produce market rhizomes, select those that are firm, plump, and free of wrinkles, soft spots, and mold. After soaking the rhizomes in water to remove any growth inhibitors, plant according to the directions provided below.

Dormant rhizomes can be potted at any time. Propagate new plants by division. Snap single fingers from turmeric seed rhizomes, leaving a few of the smallest fingers on the large, main seed piece. Allow the severed tissue to scab over by placing fingers on racks with good air circulation for several days. Plant the fingers on top of growing medium, with the growth buds facing up; then cover with the growing medium one to two inches deep.

Some farmers in temperate climates utilize pre-sprouting and grow tunnels to stretch the active growing season as long as possible for best yields and shelf life of these crops. Pre-sprouting is unnecessary for growing immature or "baby" turmeric.

Harvest of potted grandmother turmeric plant with many rhizomes—to be divided for culinary uses and replanting. Note the many rootlets on the rhizomes. *Pat Kenny*

If pre-sprouting is desired, plant the prepared rhizomes in shallow containers of moistened pasteurized potting medium, clean sand or coco coir (made from the outer husks of coconuts). Place them on a thermostat-regulated heat mat or other consistently warm surface. Maintain high humidity with mist. Turmeric requires 86°F and sprouts within 31 days.

After the buds sprout, remove the plants from the heat mat and keep them above 50°F, with strong light, until all danger of frost has passed.

In our greenhouse, pots that have sat on the bench, seemingly devoid of life during winter months, send up strong green shoots in late spring, when they are good and ready. In zones 6 and 7, new leaves appear by the end of May.

We carry over rhizomes from our plants from year to year. In early winter the healthiest rhizomes, free of any rot, are selected for next year's crop. The hands are divided and transplanted into fresh, dry potting medium to cure. They remain dry and dormant in a cool, dark area that remains a constant 50° to 57°F until spring.

Wait to move the rhizomes or sprouted plants outside until after all danger of frost has passed and soil temperature is above 50°F. Plant the fingers one foot apart so that new growth has room to expand. During the summer, gardeners can grow turmeric in large pots with humus-rich, peat or wood bark-based potting medium, with compost added or coco coir medium. Garden soil must have excellent drainage and be weed-free, consistently moist, and rich in organic matter. Plant-based mulch or hilling with soil will retain moisture and suppress weed competition.

A walled or patio garden room that is protected from high winds, with other tropical plants, is a perfect place to grow specimens of these herbs. Turmeric shoots love high humidity and filtered sun. However, according to studies at North Carolina State University, rhizome production is increased by full sun, though the leaves will likely display burned spots. Online image searches illustrate that these plants are grown in both full sun and shade.

According to the Agricultural Resource Council, turmeric's world market sales were estimated at $4.3 billion in 2020 and are projected to keep growing.

Harvesting and preserving

The leaves of turmeric will stand through the summer. Then, as daylight hours shorten and temperatures get cooler in the fall, the leaves begin to turn yellow and wither. Just before outside night temperatures fall below 55°F, bring the plants in from the garden to a sunny window. After the leaves have died completely, it is time to harvest baby rhizomes to use in the kitchen. Wash them thoroughly, air-dry and then store in a paper bag in the refrigerator crisper drawer. Do not seal them in plastic bags, as this encourages mold and will spoil the crop.

For longer storage, turmeric rhizomes can be frozen whole in freezer containers, or grated and frozen in containers. Susan has also grated it, added oil just to cover and frozen it—she uses organic coconut oil—and then scoops out a spoonful as needed for golden milk, curry, soup, etc.

Blue turmeric (*Curcuma aeruginosa*) growing in Henry Flowers' garden in Brenham, Texas, zone 8a, where he grows a collection of Zingiberaceae outdoors, year-round. *Susan Belsinger*

Turmeric flavor and use

When biting into fresh turmeric, the first taste is aromatic, much like fresh ginger without the burn. There is a slight astringency and pleasant bitterness. Tina enjoys holding a short piece in her mouth, giving it a chew from time to time as an oral change of pace from chewing gum. Her fingers turn orange from peeling the skin away although her teeth remain white.

The bright orange-yellow color of fresh turmeric is an indication of carotenoids, which are naturally occurring pigments that give it the characteristic color. Curcumin is the crude extract of turmeric rhizomes, which contain pigments that are the deep yellow color of egg yolk. This characteristic is used commercially to color foods including canned fish, cereals, chips, curry powder, dairy products, margarine, mustard, pastries, popcorn and more. Turmeric is a traditional colorant for textiles in India and has long been used in trade for dyes, both for cloth and skin.

Left, container-grown Zingiberaceae at peak of summer; Right, the same plants in late fall (before frost) with yellowing leaves—heading toward dormancy—time to harvest. *Susan Belsinger*

Medicinal virtues

In tropical Asian countries, *Curcuma* has been used medicinally for centuries. It was not until the early 1990s that western herbalists began to seriously consider using this medicinal plant.

Turmeric is antibacterial, antifungal, antioxidant, anti-inflammatory, astringent, choleretic, cholagogue (stimulates bile production in the liver), hepatotoxic, vermifuge, and antispasmodic. It is strengthening and warming to the body.

According to WebMD.com, turmeric is possibly effective for treating hay fever, depression (when used with other anti-depressants), high cholesterol, osteoarthritis (in the knees) and itching (from kidney disease and mustard gas exposure). There is insufficient, though promising, early research for the effective treatment with turmeric or isolated curcumin extracts, of Alzheimer's disease, eye inflammation, colorectal cancer, bypass surgery, Crohn's disease, diabetes, joint pain, prostate cancer, rheumatoid arthritis, and ulcerative colitis.

Pregnant women, nursing mothers, people with gall bladder issues, who are taking blood thinners or who are prone to kidney stones should avoid medicinal doses of curcumin for an extended length of time. Always report the herbs that you are taking on a regular basis to your health care professional.

Susan Belsinger and **Tina Marie Wilcox** first met in 1996 when Susan went to present two herb programs at the Ozark Folk Center in Mountain View, Arkansas. Susan arrived with a national reputation for culinary artistry, gardening expertise, and excellence in presenting, writing, and garden photography. Tina Marie as herbalist, interpreter, herb event coordinator and head gardener for the Heritage Herb Garden had developed a niche for wild foods, native herbs, organic gardening, and folk life. Having herbs and gardening in common—they hit it off—as so many of us herbies naturally do. Over the years, gardening from their respective homes, Susan in Maryland, and Tina Marie in Arkansas, their long-distance friendship evolved. They have been collaborating on presentations together, as well as writing articles for national publications like *The Herb Companion* and *Herbs for Health*. With infectious enthusiasm, both women love sharing their knowledge of herbs, plants, and gardening with like-minded people and learning from them in return.

This turmeric plant has been in captivity in a pot for 4 years and it is breaking free. *Tina Marie Wilcox*

Lucie showing off Harbinger Farm turmeric rhizomes—a healthy plant yields about 1 to 1 1/2 pounds.

Harbinger Farm Photo Essay
Turmeric: From Seed to Harvest

Lucie and Matt Day

HF ordered their organic "seed" for both ginger and turmeric from Biker Dude at Puna Organics, (www.hawaiianorganicginger.com); this variety is 'Hawaii Red'.

These 'Hawaii Red' rhizomes were started in February (in Oregon greenhouse, zone 8b), in coarse potting soil mix used for starts, in 4 1/2-inch pots.

Turmeric takes a bit longer to sprout than ginger, about 3 to 4 weeks. Periodic liquid feed is applied once sprouts emerge comprised of fish emulsion, kelp and a diverse blend of essential micronutrients. These plants with at least two to four healthy leaves are ready to transplant into the unheated hoophouse in the field once the risk of frost has passed, usually late May. Prior to transplant, soil is amended with biochar and pelletized chicken manure (4-3-2 NPK).

Bagheera cruising the allée of turmeric and ginger plants in the hoophouse. Sides are rolled up for ventilation during the day in hot weather. About 2 to 3 months post-transplant, beds were top-dressed with compost and hilled.

Plants are watered with an in-line irrigation system. About once a month, foliar feed with desalinated sea water (magnesium and boron); alternated every two weeks with fertigation of fish emulsion and kelp. They are spaced about 6 inches apart and grow to about 3 to 4 feet in height. Occasionally a plant will flower in late summer, though uncommon in a temperate climate.

In October/November, once leaves start to turn yellow, it is time to begin harvest. Turmeric harvest is a good 4 weeks later than ginger. Generally, the foliage is topped and composted when harvesting the rhizomes, however Lucie and Matt left the whole plant for this photo op.

One plant of this golden variety from Azure (azurestandard.com), about 3 to 4 feet in height, yields quite a hefty cluster of rhizomes. These are dug out carefully and laterally, rather than pulled upward, to keep rhizomes intact.

Rhizomes are washed well and broken into retail-friendly finger pieces for farmers' market sales and CSA boxes.

Washed and trimmed rhizomes ready for market day. Rhizomes are stored in the walk-in cooler for 1 to 2 weeks in an air-tight container lined with kraft paper to control humidity. Otherwise freeze for long-term storage.

Matt and Lucie Day hail from the east coast—Maryland, to be exact. They met while working at a farm-to-table restaurant in Baltimore, and eventually decided to take a leap of faith and move to the west coast in 2013, without any real plan in mind. It didn't take long for them to fall in love with the wild and rugged left side of the country, where they learned to become stewards of the land through various growing experiences. They set out to find a little slice of paradise to call their own and ended up in Myrtle Creek, Oregon, in the spring of 2020. As they continue to transform Harbinger Farm into a permaculture-minded, food-growing space, they aim to provide their community with a reliable source of fresh produce—with only organic inputs, of course. Follow this pair on their farming ventures, and be sure to hang on tight through all the bumps and brambles!

https://www.harbinger-farm.com/
https://www.instagram.com/harbinger.farm
https://www.facebook.com/p/harbinger-farm-100081260057100/

worth its weight in gold
natural herbal ally
yellow rhizome dye

Susan Belsinger

UNG • GOLDEN
urmeric
$5.50 /1/4 LB
YOUNG • FRESH
gingerroot
$5.50 /1/4 LB
fermented
hot Sauce
$10

UmPqua Valley Farmers' Market in Roseburg, Oregon—Harbinger Farm's rhizomes are always a sellout. *All photos by Lucie and Matt Day.*

Gert Coleman: "A turmeric spell jar helps to visualize good fortune streaming into your life like sunlight." *Alicia Mann*

Root Magic
The Ceremonial Uses of Turmeric

Gert Coleman

Turmeric (*Curcuma longa*) has reached such esteemed status worldwide as a culinary spice and health supplement that we may not be aware just how magical, spiritual, and symbolic it has been considered through the ages.

Since ancient times, in India, much of Asia, and the Pacific Islands, this vibrant yellow-orange rhizome has brightened cooking, advanced healing, and symbolized abundance, protection, and spiritual energy. In both ceremonial and everyday use, turmeric's mystical properties help to cleanse physical environments as well as the human aura. Priests in temples and folks in ordinary homes alike have used turmeric to sanctify their spaces and guard against malevolent influences. Turmeric's golden root has been ground, dried, and mixed into ceremonial powders and pastes to honor deities, anoint brides and grooms, and add symbolic color to festive occasions. So prized a commodity, the Chinese Yu tribes once sent turmeric as tribute to the emperor.

Color as Symbol

Colors are believed to have vibrational energies, able to influence mood and perception, and connect the physical and spiritual realms. Turmeric's brilliant, long-lasting yellow color symbolizes purity, prosperity, and new beginnings. Think of how golden sunlight visibly improves mood and outlook after a week of rain and gray skies. We are ready to start again with new energy and a positive outlook.

At festive occasions like baby showers, weddings, and holidays, yellow suggests the joy of new beginnings while symbolizing abundance, divinity, and fertility—think golden coins, religious halos, and sunflowers. Many Indian and Asian celebrations involve wearing yellow, carrying yellow or golden objects, painting walls yellow, and decorating religious statues with turmeric paste and flowers. Asian art often incorporates yellow hues to accentuate themes of tradition, beauty, and cultural identity. For me, bright yellows help to catch the eye, capture the imagination, and offset darker hues. Yellow has also been prized as a color of intellectual stimulation, favored in children's nurseries and classrooms. In my yoga class, we mentally surround ourselves with golden light as both protection and connection to our spirituality.

Turmeric, once called Indian Saffron, provides deep yellow, gold, and orange hues that are used in everything from priestly robes and festive garments to sacred icons, to foster well-being and mystical ambience. Because the color yellow is believed to ward off evil spirits and protect against negative energies, dried turmeric root can be carried for protection, worn in amulets, fashioned into jewelry, or ground into powder and sprinkled, burned, or infused in water.

One simple way to clear a space of dark influences (after an argument or an unpleasant encounter, for example) is to disperse turmeric water or dried powder around the home. Its antiseptic qualities make it ideal for sickrooms to dispel odors and germs. In Hawaii, where turmeric is known as *olena*, the ground root is mixed with salt and sometimes dried *ti* leaf (*Cordyline fruticosa*), a local plant used in traditional magic and medicine, to be strewn throughout the area to be purified. Turmeric by itself may also be scattered on the floor or around a sacred circle to guard against threats.

Turmeric is believed to invite financial stability as well as increased harmony into family life, so be sure to get some in each corner, cupboard, and closet as well as over each threshold, opening, and portal, to be thorough in your intention. Scattering turmeric powder onto the floor and into corners of a new car, boat, or tractor may encourage safety and protection against bad drivers, accidents, and road rage.

Be aware that working with turmeric can stain many surfaces. Slicing fresh turmeric root stains my wooden cutting board. I now slice it on a paper plate instead. Scrubbing with a non-abrasive cleanser or rubbing with lemon juice or parsley can reduce the yellow stain on the cutting board, but only time and repeated cleanings get rid of it entirely.

You could also hang turmeric beads from the rearview mirror to scent and protect your vehicle. Turmeric's main ingredient, curcumin, is believed to have calming qualities, helpful during traffic jams and stressful driving trips.

In one Hindu tradition, *Ganesha* idols are created with a claylike paste of turmeric, flour, and gum arabic, decorated with cloves for eyes. Revered as the remover of obstacles, Lord Ganesha is also honored as the god of wisdom and all beginnings, and the patron of the arts and sciences. Turmeric adds an auspicious and spiritual layer of meaning, due to its associations with prosperity, good health, and good fortune. The act of creating a Ganesha idol is both a devotional and meditative practice, and a good one to do with children to prepare for festivities (https://shiftychevre.com/how-to-make-ganesha-with-turmeric/).

Turmeric beads, made from ground turmeric mixed with water and dried, or carved from large roots and dried, can be carried in pockets, or strung together as necklaces and used as talismans to shield against physical and psychological harm, warding off evil spirits or undetected negativity resonating in public places. This might be a useful de-stressing strategy for increasing personal resilience, especially if worn daily.

In southwestern India, turmeric, or *mala*, beads, in a configuration of 108 beads plus one larger *guru* bead, are used for counting prayers (*pujas*) and as part of mindfulness and meditative practices (*japa*). The number 108 has mystical associations, most noteworthy the 108 letters of the Sanskrit alphabet. Mala beads can also be worn as spiritual necklaces and given as gifts.

Turmeric's mystical associations truly intrigue me because I grew up in a very Catholic household, where rosaries (once made of powdered dried roses and water) were carried in pockets and purses, kept in night table drawers for easy praying at night, and hung from mirrors, lamps, and rearview mirrors for the Blessed Mother's protection. The nuns who taught us in school wore long black rosaries from their belts, the wooden crucifix swinging against cream-colored habits as they strode by us. We dipped our hands in holy water both at church and at home and followed the colors associated with liturgical seasons. Goldenrod is blooming at the time I write this and I admire its symbolic turmeric-golden, sunshine-filled aura each time I walk my hills and yellow fields, filling my soul with life and promise, abundance and divinity, and a protective sense of place.

Healing Rituals

Bathing in sacred waters—from rivers and ponds to baths—has long been a spiritual practice on the Indian continent and in many cultures. Turmeric-infused bath water enhances well-being with its emblematic color and healing properties. By strengthening the body's energy field and aura, soaking in turmeric water improves physical health and attracts positive energy.

Western herbalism suggests taking a turmeric bath at the first signs of a cold or flu. To running water, add two to four tablespoons turmeric powder and one teaspoon cayenne powder (optional). Stir well, and soak for about twenty minutes. Be careful not to get the bath water in your eyes: the cayenne may sting. Then dry off, dress warmly, and get into bed under several covers and rest. It will make you sweat and so is very effective for breaking colds, fever, and flu (Tierra 196). You can exchange the cayenne for three tablespoons of warming dried ginger powder or an inch or two of thinly sliced fresh ginger root, but I'd still keep the bathwater out of my eyes. Drinking ginger-turmeric tea will further ease symptoms, particularly if your muscles ache. Be warned that turmeric can stain porcelain baths so be prepared to scrub the tub afterwards.

Chakras, a concept that originated in Hindu and Buddhist traditions, represent energy centers in the body, imagined as discs or wheels that radiate energy. Think of them as power centers that influence and manifest physical and spiritual well-being. If life is out of balance—stress, environmental factors, money worries, family issues, politics, social pressures, emotional upsets; the list is endless—the chakras will reflect that imbalance.

Each chakra is associated with a color. Turmeric's yellow and gold tones are believed to help balance the third chakra (there are seven), located in the solar plexus, which controls one's sense of identity, confidence, and personal growth. The solar plexus is where we might repress emotions and carry tension. If you have a "gut feeling" about something, that could be an intuitive sign your chakras need balancing. Medicinally, turmeric has long been used to heal gut issues. Psychologically and topically, turmeric's characteristic color comes into play here: Yellow, particularly in the natural form of a flower or spice, offers courage and strength to face challenges. Bathing in turmeric water, or even taking a footbath with turmeric water, can create a time to rest, relax, meditate, and reconnect.

For a chakra-healing bath, add a few tablespoons of turmeric powder or several slices of fresh rhizome to your bathwater as the water is running. Medicinally, turmeric has been known to ease skin issues and muscle pain, and to help individuals relax when needed. Absorbed through the bath water, turmeric's healing properties help detoxify the body by flushing out impurities, thus reinforcing the idea of symbolic cleansing. Once immersed in the bath, concentrate on the golden yellow color surrounding you, slowly breathe in and out to release any blocked energy, and visualize joy and good fortune coming into your life.

If a bath is too much trouble or inconvenient, simply meditating on a piece of turmeric or a string of turmeric beads might help realign unbalanced energies, dispel negative influences, and promote inner peace and a sense of protection. For deeper insights before meditation, mix half a teaspoon of dried turmeric powder with a small amount of water or coconut oil into a paste and apply to the middle of the forehead, where the third eye chakra is believed to be, to open new channels of understanding.

Another healing, calming ritual involves the light and warmth of candles. During a bath or meditation, or simply as a pleasant ritual itself, burning yellow candles can help to initiate new beginnings, attract prosperity or protection, or restore balance and build resilience. To enhance the candle's power, first etch or carve small symbols or words into the wax to spell out the intention. Further strengthen the ritual by rubbing a small amount of turmeric powder onto the symbols. Mixing the turmeric with your own saliva first can further "charge" or personalize the ritual. Light the candle and focus on the intention, breathing gently and rhythmically. As you breathe, visualize golden light filling your space, and by extension, your life, your essential being, your soul, with positive energy (*Buddhatooth.com*).

A strong infusion of turmeric water can also be used to cleanse ritual objects, enhancing their color vibrations and mystical energies. And, if you have extra, sprinkling turmeric-infused water around the house is a good way to welcome guests, as well as shift the energy once they leave your premises.

A spell jar is a creative, more discreet method to use turmeric's transformative power to focus an intention without having to clean the bathtub or have the car smell like turmeric. Fill a small, clean jar with a mixture of dried turmeric powder or dried turmeric slices (not fresh as they may rot), then add a few symbolic yellow things like gold coins, golden pebbles, dried golden leaves (gingko, for example), dried yellow flowers (calendula, goldenrod, marigolds, roses, tansy, yarrow), or yellow-hued gemstones (citrine, topaz, sapphire). As you add each item, visualize your intention (protection, good fortune, etc.) and say it out loud as a prayer. Be sure to put the spell jar where you will see it. Each time you pass it, try to visualize good fortune streaming into your life like sunlight.

Festivities, Blessings, and Light Over Darkness

Diwali, the Indian Festival of Light, celebrates the triumph of light over darkness, goodness over evil, and knowledge over ignorance. Turmeric's bright yellow qualities add to the celebrations in foods and rituals. In the fall, families and friends gather together for several days of feasting, exchanging gifts, enjoying fireworks, parades, and a ritual oil bath (with turmeric, of course). Diwali often involves new clothes and decorating; yellow and orange are the colors of choice, inviting abundance, prosperity, and auspicious new beginnings.

During Diwali, many gods are honored, but Lakshmi, the four-armed goddess whose name means "fortunate woman" is especially invoked as the goddess of beauty, fertility, prosperity, sovereignty, and wealth, and for her affinity with the colors yellow and red. In India, Lakshmi is a very popular girl's name, associated with auspiciousness and good fortune.

At the feast, turmeric colors and flavors curries, condiments, golden milk

Gert Coleman: *"Diwali*, the Indian Festival of Light, celebrates the triumph of light over darkness, goodness over evil, and knowledge over ignorance." *Wikimedia Creative Commons*

drinks, chai teas, and many sweet desserts. Turmeric joins other aromatic spices symbolizing abundance for Diwali celebrations: cardamom, cinnamon, cloves, fennel, and ginger. These blend well together and aid in digestion.

In Indonesia, turmeric is a key element in harvest festivals symbolizing gratitude for the crops and the abundance of the earth. Turmeric is often offered in prayers and placed on altars for continued prosperity and good fortune.

Possibly the most popular—and public—use of turmeric's golden power dazzles in the colorful, joyous pre-wedding *haldi* tradition. In Hindu, *haldi* means turmeric and the ceremony is called the *pithi* ceremony or *Haldi ki rasam*.

A day or two prior to the ceremony, friends and family gather to make a fragrant paste of ground turmeric, ground sandalwood, and rosewater. Yogurt, almond oil, gram flour, or fuller's earth may also be used to accommodate different skin types.

During the ceremony, the elders, wearing yellow and orange attire, apply turmeric paste to the bride and groom's face, neck, hands, and feet, using mango leaves, blades of grass, brushes, or wands. They offer congratulations, blessings, and advice as they go. Then other family members and friends get their turns, with more heartfelt wishes for love, prosperity, and happiness. Singing, dancing, and praying are all part of the tradition, with much laughter and joy, providing a good start for the bride and groom.

Turmeric's bright color and healing energies are intended to frighten away evil spirits, ease pre-weddings jitters, invoke blessings, and prepare the couple for their new life together. Since ancient times, turmeric paste has been identified as an antiseptic solution and often applied for radiant and blemish-free skin, so the bridal couple should look their best on their wedding day.

While the haldi ceremony has been predominantly a Hindu wedding ritual, the popularity of Bollywood movies has spread this colorful trend to other cultures too. Numerous wedding websites are devoted to the ritual, with suggestions for gifts to participants, including small jars of the turmeric paste to be brought home as souvenirs.

Turmeric also stains the skin. According to WeddingsinAthens.com, you can try one of these methods to remove turmeric stains, after which you would rinse well with water. Rub skin with olive oil or coconut oil; soak a washcloth in milk and gently rub skin with it; mix equal parts water and apple cider vinegar and rub gently to remove stains; or use a honey and lemon mask to remove haldi stains.

Turmeric has become increasingly popular in skincare products. When mixed with other botanicals and modern-day emollients, turmeric's healing traits can be accessed without its staining abilities, according to *Vogue* magazine. One cited ginger-turmeric oil extract costs $80 per fluid ounce. (See Janice Cox's article on page 147 to make your own turmeric skincare products.)

Turmeric, 2026 Herb of the Year!

Turmeric can clearly bring joy and healing to any occasion, as well as fragrance, flavor, and color. Wearing turmeric jewelry, carrying turmeric talismans, sprinkling turmeric-infused water around the house, decorating with shades of turmeric-yellow for symbolic and festive significance—these may seem like ancient and arcane practices. However, these very actions underscore the contemporary emphasis on turmeric for our overall health and well-being.

As we live through stressful times, embracing turmeric may be a very colorful and healing solution. Almost every angle from which we consider the "Golden Spice of India," we can celebrate turmeric's cultural, culinary, magical, medicinal, and mystical qualities.

References

Balagam, Iman. "Turmeric Skin Care Without the Yellow Stains? Yes, It's Possible." *Vogue*. August 19, 2025. https://www.vogue.com/article/turmeric-skincare. Accessed 8/20/25.

Bartram, Thomas. *Bartram's Encyclopedia of Herbal Medicine*. Robinson, 1998.

Bown, Deni. *Herbal: The Essential Guide to Herbs for Living*. Barnes & Noble, 2001.

Chesson, Brian. "What Does Turmeric Symbolize? Discovering Its Cultural and Spiritual Significance." 1/2/2025. *Knowbies.com*. https://knowbies.com/what-does-turmeric-symbolize/. Accessed 1/27/25.

Dalby, Andrew. *Dangerous Tastes: The Story of Spices*. U of Calif, 2000. 139.

Dalton, David. *Stars of the Meadow*. LindisfarneBooks, 2006.

de la Tour, Shatoiya. *Earth Mother Herbal*. Fair Winds Press, 2002.

Elrod, Daniel. "Turmeric Flower Meaning, Symbolism & Spiritual Significance." 1/27/25. *Foliage Friend*. https://foliagefriend.com/turmeric-flower-meaning/. Accessed 1/27/25.

Grieve, Mrs. M. *A Modern Herbal*. Barnes & Noble, 1996 (1931). 822-823.

"Haldi Ceremony–Explained in Detail." *Brajamandala.com*. https://brajamandala.com/hindu-ceremonies-explained-in-detail/. Accessed 7/8/25.

Hall, MacKenzie. "Warriors against disease." 1/12/2013. *Staten Island Advance*.

"How to Make Ganesha with Turmeric?" *Shiftychevre*. 12/1/2024. https://shiftychevre.com/how-to-make-ganesha-with-turmeric/. Accessed 8/21/25.

Krondl, Michael. *The Taste of Conquest: The Rise and Fall of the Three Great Cities of Spice*. Ballantine, 2007.

Marano, Hara Estroff. "Spices have a tasty array of health benefits." 2/11/13. *Staten Island Advance*.

Mulherin, Jennifer. *The Macmillan Treasury of Spices & Natural Flavorings*. Macmillan, 1988. 92-93.

Polizzi, Nick. "The Ancient Art of Chakra Bathing." 7/14/2025. *The Sacred Science*. https://www.thesacredscience.com/the-ancient-art-of-chakra-bathing/. Accessed 7/15/25.

Shih-Chen, Li. *Chinese Medicinal Herbs: A Modern Edition of a Classic Sixteenth-Century Manual*. Dover, 2003. 138-140.

"Spiritual Benefits of Putting Turmeric in Bath Water in Hinduism." *Hindu Blog.* https://www.hindu-blog.com/2013/09/spiritual-benefits-of-putting-turmeric.html. Accessed 7/11/25.

Tierra, Lesley. *A Kid's Herb Book.* Robert D. Reed Publ, 2000. 196.

Turner, Jack. *Spice: The History of a Temptation.* Knopf, 2004.

Kohler, Christine. "What is Haldi Ceremony in Hindu Wedding?" *Weddings in Athens.com.* https://weddingsinathens.com/what-is-haldi-ceremony-in-hindu-wedding.html. Accessed 7/8/25.

Wood, Matthew. *The Earthwise Herbal: A Complete Guide to Old World Medicinal Plants.* North Atlantic, 2008. 228-230.

"5 Spices that can bring wealth this Diwali." 10/26/2025. *Times of India.* https://timesofindia.indiatimes.com/life-style/food-news/5-spices-that-can-bring-wealth-this-diwali/articleshow/114580266.cms. Accessed 7/14/25.

"5 Surprising Spiritual Uses of Turmeric That Will Transform Your Practice." 8/14/24. *Buddhatooth.com.* https://buddhatooth.com/spiritual-uses-of-turmeric/#google_vignette. Accessed 1/27/25.

"20 Ancient Amulets for Protection from Negative Energy." *ReflectEvolve.* 7/6/2023. https://www.outofstress.com/amulets-for-protection/. Accessed 8/20/25.

Herbal educator, writer, gardener, editor, and herb enthusiast, **Gert Coleman** loves, grows, eats, and reads avidly about herbs. Retired professor of English, she lives on 100+ acres in Central New York, growing herbs, flowers, trees, and at-risk native plants with her husband and dog.

As an herbal educator, she has taught humorous and informative programs for all ages at parks, museums, and conferences; helped maintain a 70' x 70' colonial herb garden for 3 decades; apprenticed with Rosemary Gladstar; compiled and edited five Herb of the Year™ books; and writes about the legends, lore, and poetry of herbs. In addition, she teaches workshops on nature writing in the wild places of New York and beyond. Gertc3456@gmail.com

Turmeric, Ancient Canoe Plant

Kathleen Connole

Turmeric (*Curcuma longa*) and Ginger (*Zingiber officinale*), both members of the family Zingiberaceae, were among the valued plants that the ancient Austronesian people carried with them as they traveled and settled across the vast reaches of the Pacific Ocean. These ancestors of the people now known as Polynesians, Melanesians, and Micronesians established the earliest maritime trade network from the Pacific islands, across the Indian Ocean, to the east coast of Africa. Turmeric, originally from Southeast Asia, has been one of the most revered plants in Chinese, Asian, and Ayurvedic medicine, and has been used for food, dye and ceremony for thousands of years.

Their migration from Taiwan began 6,000 years before present; by 3,300 years ago they had spread from island to island in the archipelagos now known as Indonesia, the Philippines, Malaysia, and Oceania, which includes Polynesia, Micronesia and Melanesia, traveling hundreds of miles at a time.

The name "Austronesian" refers to the language family of these people. The word comes from "austral" meaning southern, and "nesia," islands. Successive generations, many of whom we now know as Polynesians, spread some 6,500 miles throughout the Indo-Pacific oceans, and today some 270 million people speak languages with their roots in ancient Austronesian.

There are over 1,200 closely related islands, including modern-day well-known Sumatra, Java, Borneo, Malaysia, Timor, New Guinea, the Mariannas, Samoa, Tahiti, New Zealand, and the Philippines. Hawaii was one of the last groups of islands to be settled by descendants of the Austronesians, around 940 to 1130 AD.

Long before the overland trade routes from China to the Red Sea, there was what is called the "maritime silk road." The people of the archipelagos of the Eastern Pacific, the area later known as the East Indies, had been trading their "forest products" with the Chinese and the people of ancient India, since the second century BCE.

The Moluccas, or "Spice Islands," a tiny group of islands, located at the intersection of Asia and Oceania, were the only place in the world where cloves, *Syzygium aromaticum,* and nutmeg, *Myristica fragrans*, naturally inhabited. The spices of the Moluccas were the most coveted and valuable of any trade item.

The Austronesian people were the world's first mariners. The earliest known group, known as the Lapita, developed sailing technologies at least 3,500 years ago specific to their needs. The voyaging canoes were large enough to hold families, their provisions, and a cargo of plants and animals, seaworthy enough to travel long distances and survive all weather conditions encountered. The Polynesians later refined the boats with wave splitters and splash boards and embellished them with carvings of symbolic cultural images.

*Camakau o*utrigger canoe, constructed entirely from the island's native trees and plant fibers, using only stone, bone, and seashell tools. *Museum of New Zealand*

The Austronesians displayed remarkable ingenuity in their boat-building and navigational skills. The outrigger boats were constructed from native trees and plant fibers, using only stone, bone, and seashell tools. The skill in the construction of these boats is truly amazing. In the article "The Ethnobotany of Ocean-going Canoes in Lau, Fiji," authors Banack and Cox describe the entire process from start to finish. They witnessed the native carpenters of the island, well known for their expertise in constructing these canoes, as they demonstrated the centuries-old craft. Twenty different species of plants were used, from the hardwood trees that grow there, to the specific woods needed from other trees for each section of the canoe, to the sennit fiber made from coconut mesocarp—used to literally stitch the pieces of wood together—to a special species of palm-like tree providing the leaves made into fabric by the women for the sails, to the sap of a specific tree used as a glue. The canoes still being made on this island are considered "the pinnacle of South Pacific craftsmanship" (Banack and Cox,1987).

These vessels made possible the settlement of the multitude of islands of the South Pacific and the maritime trade route across the Indian Ocean to India and the east coast of Africa. The outrigger canoes were still in use in the late 1800s and written about by Ernest Way Elkington in his book *The Savage South Seas*: "…it consists of three canoes lashed together and boarded over. On these boards is a kind of barn, cut down and spread out considerably. This is used both for shelter and for carrying the pots and articles of barter. From the centre of this raft-like barge the two enormous sails project straight into the air; the two horn-like points of the top are decorated with long streamers… [These boats are] used for long trips, and carry big crews, being often loaded to their full carrying capacity" (p. 57).

By 1778, when Captain Cook was on his third voyage across the Pacific, the Austronesians were inhabiting islands stretching from New Zealand in the south, to Hawaii and Easter Island in the east, to Madagascar in the west. According to Brian Lavery in *The Conquest of the Ocean*, Cook marveled that they had accomplished this in simple boats without the aid of charts or compasses. Joseph Banks, Cook's naturalist, observed: "They (the boats) are frequently upset but the people are almost amphibious and care little for such accidents… [They are] such good swimmers that only seals can be compared with them" (Lavery, 2013).

"They approached the open ocean with great respect; no other culture embraced the open sea so fully." Predictable, seasonal winds, an intimate knowledge of the ocean's currents, and the tropical climate, in which the sun and stars were most often visible, were taken advantage of by these primitive navigators. "The paths of the stars and the rhythms of the ocean guided them by night, and the color of the sky and the sun, the shapes of the clouds, and the direction from which the swells were coming, guided them by day" (Clark, *Nova Newsletter*, www.pbs.org).

The Pacific Ocean is the largest geographical feature on earth, covering nearly one-third of its surface. Most of the islands being discussed here have equatorial tropical climates, except for Hawaii (which is north of the equator), and New Zealand and Easter Island; these are temperate and subtropical. The geology of the islands changes from west to east. The western islands are formed from "continental-type" rocks and are thought to be part of the ancient super continent Gondwanaland, that split apart 167 million years ago. Over most of the Pacific basin the islands are *oceanic*, meaning that they are composed of ancient volcanic basalt rock, and range in age from very recent to almost 20 million years old. The "high islands" are volcanic domes; the highest is Hawaii with two peaks over 13,000 feet.

Over millions of years other islands have eroded to at or below sea level, called "low islands" that over time have become surrounded by coral reefs; today these are known as *atolls*. They are covered by a limestone cap up to hundreds of meters thick, above the original basalt base. The geology affects the types of plant life to be found naturally on these islands. The atolls are of "superb beauty...[with] azure and turquoise-blue central lagoons with chains of coral and sand islets...strung out like pearls of a necklace along all or part of the perimeter...in stark contrast to harsh living conditions that allow only a limited number of terrestrial plant species" (Whistler, p.2-3).

The Austronesians wisely carried with them "canoe plants," plants so important to them for food, fiber, medicine, and ritual, that they fit them into their outrigger canoes along with their entire families and necessities. They would settle along the coastal areas where they found favorable conditions. Survival at the beginning depended solely upon food from the sea and whatever few native plants grew there, for months or even years, until the propagules (seeds, rhizomes and/or cuttings) that they brought with them became established.

Some of the plants that they transported and planted wherever they landed include: candlenut, taro, breadfruit, jackfruit, yams, sweet potatoes, bamboo, gourds, coconut, Job's tears, citrus, *Ficus* species, banana, rice, *Piper* species, sugar cane, arrowroot, and the Zingiberaceae family, including *Alpinia galanga*, galangal; *Curcuma longa*, turmeric, *C. zedoaria*, white turmeric, *Zingiber officinale*, ginger; and *Z. zerumbet*, shampoo ginger. Many of these plants have in common the fact that they are propagated from rhizomes and provided staple carbohydrate-containing foods. Others could be propagated by seed. Both forms could be carried over long distances and remain viable. The fact that sweet potatoes were an important food crop for these people since ancient times strongly suggests that they were able to cross the Pacific and obtain them from the plant's native land of the Andes mountains of South America. The latest scientific genetic studies have confirmed that there was contact between the people of Easter Island and South America 19 to 23 generations ago, between 1300 and 1500 AD (Handwerk, B. www. smithsonianmagazine.com).

The Austronesians and their descendants were gatherers and gardeners rather than agriculturists. To succeed at cultivating their chosen plants, they had to possess horticultural knowledge of each one's growing requirements. They took advantage of the climate and growing conditions in the islands where they settled. They had no beasts of burden. In addition to the plants listed, they cultivated fruit and nut trees, and they had known how to grow rice and millet since coming from Taiwan. They possessed an intimate knowledge of the plants that they tended and how to propagate them and keep them alive as they traveled from island to island. The indigenous plants already growing there were also made use of, in multiple and ingenious ways.

There is little archeological evidence of plant use due to the tropical climate that ensures rapid decomposition. Remnants of tools used in gardening and food processing have been found and provide clues about the plants that they used. However, there are descendants of these people who have continued to grow and use the same plants; the knowledge of their uses has been passed down through the generations. The strongest evidence is the proliferation and naturalization of these plants throughout the areas that were settled by the Austronesians.

In addition to food plants, canoe plants were important sources of materials for medicine, ritual, plaiting, cordage, clothing, housing, canoe-building, fishing, crafts, ornamentation, musical instruments, and toys.

"If a plant had not proved its usefulness … it is unlikely that it would have been given space in canoes laden with people, pigs, dogs, chickens, water, and food stocks to be eaten en route" (Abbott, 1992).

The plants were wrapped in layers of moist moss, leaves, or *kapa* cloth, and hung from the roof of the canoe's hut, or stowed in gourds, to safely make the journey across the open, storm-tossed seas.

Of the 50 to 60 known canoe plants, it is now known that only about 26 made it as far as the Hawaiian archipelago, which is the farthest to the north and one of the last to be settled. These plants "conveyed the entire world of the original Hawaiians: their nourishment, their handicrafts, their medicines, and the foundation of their life of the spirit" (Stein, M. www.mauimagazine.net).

Turmeric, *Curcuma longa* L. (syn. *C. domestica*) was surely one of these canoe plants, known in Hawai'i as *'ōlena, "yellow."* There are names for this plant in countless Polynesian languages, usually meaning yellow. This species of *Curcuma* can no longer be found growing in the wild; it rarely blooms or produces viable seeds. It is easily propagated from its rhizome, that readily sprouts given the right conditions.

Ethnobotanist Arthur Whistler has spent over 40 years studying the vegetation, ecology, flora, and medicinal plant uses of Polynesia. Whistler observed in his studies of the peoples of Polynesia that prior to the 1700s, as they were virtually isolated from the rest of the world, nearly all European accounts described them as "healthy and vigorous … [and] amazingly free of infectious diseases" (p. 12).

He also noted that their beliefs attributed internal illnesses to supernatural causes, thus those were treated by prayer and intercession by priests. Plants as medicine were used for cuts and wounds, fractures, sprains, rashes, skin infections, burns, digestive issues, ear, mouth, and throat infections. Of course, the lack of immunity to European infectious diseases wiped out thousands of indigenous Polynesian people.

The primary use for *C. longa* in most cultures was to produce the yellow dye. In his earlier book, *Polynesian Herbal Medicine*, Whistler describes the traditional method, still in use in Western Polynesia: "an extract from the grated *Curcuma* rhizome is placed in coconut shell cups or bamboo sections, baked in an earth oven, producing the yellow powder … The dye was formerly used for coloring *tapa* cloth, for cosmetic purposes, and for painting newborn babies and their mothers." He also mentions that a sailor marooned on Tongo in the early 1800s used "turmeric powder mixed with coconut oil and smeared onto his body as insulation from the cold" (Whistler, 1992).

Whistler cites the historic Polynesian medicinal uses of *Curcuma longa*: used in an ointment applied to wounds, sores and rashes (including shingles), to treat gonorrhea, diabetes, urinary infections and incontinence; the juice expressed to treat ear and sinus ailments. Current uses also include turmeric's esteemed value as a condiment, and its use to scent "sweet oil" for purification purposes. Most medicinal uses refer to the rhizomes; however, on some coral atolls, where there was little soil, the plants did not produce them in enough quantity or size. The turmeric leaves were used there as medicine, to treat coughs, sore throats, and in vapor baths for fever (Kikusawa, 2007).

There is much information on '*ōlena*, as turmeric is known and revered in Hawaii. It can be found growing there in moist, forested valleys up to 3,000 feet; often growing in large clumps—evidence of past cultivation. Historically young roots were steamed to provide light-yellow dye; older roots were used to make a golden or deep orange color. The dye was painted onto the *kapa* cloth, a thin and very soft cloth, that was felted from the inner bark of the paper mulberry, rather than woven. It is interesting to note that the curcumin in turmeric "has a strong affinity for binding with [natural plant] fibers" and that the antimicrobial and anti-inflammatory properties of curcumin present in the dyed fabric might be beneficial to those with sensitive skin or allergies (Fowler, 2024).

The various but similar techniques used to process turmeric rhizomes for dye are described in *Plants of the Canoe People*. The simplest method observed was to mix the gratings with water to produce the saffron yellow color, known as *lega* in western Polynesia and *lena* in eastern Polynesia. One example involved placing the gratings in water, straining, letting it settle, taking the remaining lower layer and baking it in coconut shells, either with hot stones or in an earth oven, then drying the resulting powder in the sun. This powder was sold in the markets to be used as a condiment or mixed with coconut oil for ceremonial and medicinal uses. Today when we want to make our own freshly ground turmeric, we can purchase dried rhizomes that have been boiled before they are dried in the sun.

Traditional medicinal applications observed to be still in use include using the juice, extracted by pounding the rhizome, then mixed with water and applied through the nasal passage to treat earaches and sinus congestion; to treat consumption, tuberculosis, bronchitis, colds and asthma. Turmeric was recognized as being anti-inflammatory and the powder mixed with coconut oil was applied to skin sores, burns, infected wounds or to stop bleeding. An infusion of the scraped rhizome was used as a potion for stomachache, ulcers, diarrhea, taken as a diuretic and used to treat urinary tract infections (Whistler, 2009).

Turmeric was believed by Hawaiian people to contain much "mana" or spiritual power. The crushed root was mixed with sea water and sprinkled by

Curcuma zedoaria. Köhlers Medizinal Pflanzen, 1890. *plantillustrations.org*

the priest, using a frond of seaweed, or a *ti* leaf, along with prayer, to remove negative energy, as a ceremony to bless a new home, or to cure illness (www. canoeplants.com/olena/html).

Curcuma zedoaria, commonly called zedoary or white turmeric, is listed in several articles that cite its use throughout India, Madagascar, Indonesia, and the Pacific Islands as food and medicine. This relative can be found growing wild in its native range, which includes southern India, Assam, Bangladesh, and eastern Himalaya. It is said to have a flavor reminiscent of mangos with an extremely bitter aftertaste. The leaves have a striking purple-red midrib, and the flower is a bright pink; it is sometimes grown as an ornamental and houseplant.

Curcuma zedoaria is listed as an "Economically Important Curcuma Species" in that section of the monograph *Turmeric The Genus Curcuma*. The article states that this species name has been often applied to "several superficially similar species." For this reason, the local uses reported by Rheede, who first described it in 1692, in its native range, are believed to be the most accurate. These included the fresh root being used to arrest inflammation of the intestines, to "purge" the blood and kidneys, and cure gonorrhea. The juice of the leaves was used as a moderate laxative. The starch extract "… is much esteemed in India … and is used as arrowroot in cakes, and as a substitute for barley starch given to children" (*Turmeric*, p. 464).

Other uses cited included young shoots and fresh young leaves as a vegetable and in salads, the rhizomes in the manufacture of liqueurs, various essences, cosmetics, and perfumes, and the dried rhizomes as a spice, mainly in bitters. The good news is that there are multiple current-day studies investigating the biological activities of the chemical constituents of *Curcuma zedoaria*, reporting that its medicinal properties have been found to include antimicrobial, anticancer, analgesic, antipyretic, antiviral, antioxidant, wound-healing, anti-inflammatory, insecticidal, and cardioprotective. There appear to be many studies especially concerning its cancer-fighting properties.

The intrepid sea-faring Austronesians settled some of the most remote parts of the world and made use of the indigenous plants that they found in addition to the essential plants that they brought with them. They were the very earliest people to establish the maritime trade routes across eight thousand miles, from Hawaii in the Pacific to Madagascar in the Indian Ocean, in their ingenious outrigger canoes … "over one thousand years before the Europeans had the knowledge or skill to sail across the Atlantic"

(Whitman, Chipper, Director of the National Tropical Botanical Garden, in the introduction to *Plants of the Canoe People*, 2009).

The study of ethnobotany in today's world of such rapid change has never been more important. The traditional uses of plants, especially in the tropics, where "the vast majority of the world's vascular plants are found … knowledge of the medicinal properties of these plants is poor compared to what is known about temperate plants … and many medical practices—not only the use of herbal medicines, but also the social interaction between healer and patient—have great value for healing" (Whistler, 1992).

References

Abbott, Isabella Alona. *Lā'au Hawai'i Traditional Uses of Hawaiian Plants*. Bishop Museum Press, 1992.

Baily, R. K. "Canoe plants of ancient Hawaii." www.canoeplants.com. Accessed 11/16/25.

Banack, A. B., and Cox, P. A. "The Ethnobotany of Ocean-Going Canoes: The Pinnacle of South Pacific Craftsmanship." *Springer Nature*, Vol. 41, No.2. Apr-Jun 1987. www.jstor/stable/4254954. Accessed 11/15/24.

Clark, Leisl. "Ancient Worlds – Polynesia's Genius Navigators." *Nova Newsletter*. https://www.pbs.org/wgbh/nova/article/polynesia-genius-navigators/. Accessed 11/12/25.

Fiji camakau. *Loius le Breton*, 1846. *Public Domain*

Dalby, Andrew. *Dangerous Tastes: The Story of Spices*. University of California Press, 2000.

Elkington, Ernest W. *The Savage South Seas*. A & C Black, 1907.

Fowler, D. "Unraveling the Roots of Turmeric Dyeing." www. turmerictrove.com/articles/the-ancient-art-of-turmeric-dyeing-in-textiles. html. Accessed 11/4/25.

Gharge, S. et al. "*Curcuma zedoaria* Rosc. Zingiberaceae: A Review of its Chemical, Pharmacological, and Biological Activities." *Future Journal of Pharmaceutical Sciences,* 2021. https://fjps.springeropen.com/track/pdf/10.1186/s43094-021-00316-1.pdf. Accessed 11/16/25.

Hamilton, Roy W. "The Legacy of Indo-Pacific Voyaging." https://fowler. ucla.edu/a-look-back-at-the-art-of -austronesians-the-legacy-of-indo-pacific-voyaging/ Accessed 2/5/23.

Handwerk, Brian. "The Polynesians." *Smithsonian Science*. https:// smithsonianmagazine.com/science-nature-native-americans-polynesians-meet-1809752691. Accessed 2/9/23.

Kikusawa, R., and Reid, L. "Proto who utilized turmeric and how?" https:// scholarspace.manoa.hawaii.edu/10125/33035/A67.2007pdf. Accessed 11-10-25.

Lavery, Brian. *The Conquest of the Ocean*. DK Publishing, 2013.

"Maritime Silk Road." https://www.en.wikipedia.org/wiki/Maritime_Silk_Road. Accessed 2/4/23.

Ravindran, P. N., Babu, K. N., and Sivaraman, K., ed. *Turmeric The Genus Curcuma*. CRC Press, 2007.

"Spice Islands (Moluccas): 250 Years of Maps (1521-1760)." https://www. lib_dbserver.princeton.edu/visual_materials/maps/websites/pacific/spice-islands-maps.html. Accessed 11/15/22.

Stein, M. "Seeds Across the Seas." www.mauimagazine.net/seeds-across-the-seas/. Accessed 8/20/25.

Turner, Jack. *Spice: The History of a Temptation*. Alfred A. Knopf, 2004.

White, Lynton Dove. *Canoe Plants of Ancient Hawaii*. https://canoeplants. com. Accessed 11/15/25.

Whistler, W. Arthur. *Plants of the Canoe People: An Ethnobotanical Voyage Through Polynesia*. National Tropical Botanical Garden, 2009.

Whistler. Dr. W. Arthur. *Polynesian Herbal Medicine*. National Tropical Botanical Garden, 1992.

Kathleen Connole joined the Ozark Folk Center Heritage Herb Garden team in 2006. Before moving to Arkansas' Buffalo River country in 2005, Kathleen earned her degree in Plant Science from the University of Missouri-Columbia and worked as a gardener and greenhouse grower at Powell Gardens and Farrand Farms in Kansas City, Missouri. During her 14 years at the Ozark Folk Center, she researched and composed interpretive signs for the plants in the Garden, helped the HH Garden team and the Herb Society of America Ozark Unit design and construct several award-winning display gardens at the Arkansas Flower and Garden Show, and presented programs about the plant explorers and the history of how plants were moved around the world at the annual HHG herbal seminars. In 2020 Kathleen retired from the Garden team due to health problems; after recovery from several surgeries, she now continues her contributions to the HHG as a volunteer, and is thrilled to be able to once again hike the hills and hollows of the Ozarks in search of waterfalls and spectacular view spots. She is a member of HSA and is a Board member and Editor of Herb of the Year books for the International Herb Association; she is currently working on *Turmeric, Herb of the Year 2026*, her 5th year as editor.

The foliage of this zedoary growing in Costa Rica has the distinctive and striking purple midrib. *Wikimedia Creative Commons*

Zedoary, *Cucurma zedoaria*, can be beautiful in the garden and can be grown as a houseplant. *Wikimedia Creative Commons*

Turmeric can be used to make beautiful botanical sun prints. *Janice Cox*

Sun Printing with Turmeric

Janice Cox

While researching turmeric recipes for this book, I stumbled upon this delightful herbal craft and it quickly became one of my favorites! Using turmeric, I have had so much fun creating sun-printed papers, cards, and even fabric.

Turmeric contains curcumin, a photosensitive compound found in the root. When mixed with rubbing alcohol, it creates a natural ink that fades in sunlight, allowing you to capture beautiful silhouettes of flowers, leaves, herbs—or any object you wish to "sun print."

Note: Turmeric ink stains everything it touches, so be sure to wear gloves and old clothes or an apron while working.

Turmeric Ink

1 teaspoon turmeric powder
4 tablespoons rubbing alcohol

In a clean glass jar with a tight-fitting lid, combine the turmeric powder and alcohol. Shake gently to mix. If desired, strain the ink through a coffee filter for a smoother consistency.

Developing Solution

After your print has been exposed to sunlight, you will need a borax rinse to bring the images to life.

1/3 cup borax powder
1 gallon water

Mix the borax and water in a large container (like a recycled milk jug) and stir until fully dissolved.

Additional Materials

Paper or fabric
Paintbrush
Glass sheet (from an old picture frame)
Board or cookie sheet
Shallow pan
Botanical materials: flower heads, leaves, herbs

Instructions

1. Paint & Dry
Using your turmeric ink, paint the entire surface of your paper or fabric. Allow it to dry completely in a dark area.

2. Arrange Your Design
Place the dried paper or fabric on a board or cookie sheet. Arrange your botanical objects on top in a pleasing pattern. Cover with a glass sheet. (For safety when working with children, use acrylic sheets or tape the glass edges.)

3. Sun Exposure
Place your setup in direct sunlight. Allow it to sit until the exposed areas fade— usually a few hours.

4. Reveal & Rinse
Bring your print indoors and remove the glass and objects. Pour the borax solution into a shallow pan and rinse your project in it. Your design will begin to appear— this is the magical part!

5. Dry & Display
Let your print dry completely. You can frame it, turn it into a card, or use it in other crafts.

Note: These prints may fade over time, so if you especially love your design you may want to make a photocopy or take a photo of it.

Janice Cox is a garden writer and natural beauty expert. She is the author of several books on the topic of DIY beauty and useful garden plants. Her most recent book is *The Natural Beauty at Home Handbook* (Ogden 2024). She was the beauty editor for *Herb Quarterly* magazine for more than twenty years and the education chair for The Herb Society of America. She is a member of The International Herb Association. Mrs. Cox loves working with plants and using them in culinary, crafting and wellness projects.

Thinner and smaller than ginger, about finger-sized, turmeric root has a distinct golden hue to its skin, and vibrant golden pith. *Gail Wood Miller*

Tempestuous Turmeric

Rosemary Roman Davis

Who first dug this luscious plant up and consumed it? Violently golden, seductively earthy, aggressively pungent and vigorously healthful, turmeric is a welcome traveler on the Spice Roads from days long gone. Native to the jungles of Southeast Asia—most sources place its botanical origin in southern India or Malaysia— turmeric came by foot, camel caravan, and ship to the Chinese, to the Assyrians, Sumerians, and even to Yemen, sub-Saharan Africa, and the Mascarene Islands by the 8th century CE. Traders may have brought it to northern India as early as the 2nd century CE. Turmeric was carried into Europe, and even traveled to Sumatra, Hawaii, Jamaica and the Amazon.

There are references to turmeric in Sanskrit texts dating its use to as much as four thousand years ago, as both a food and a solar symbol in religious rituals. India, specifically the southern state of Tamil Nadu, is currently the world's largest producer of *Curcuma longa*, the most commonly grown variety out of thirty species in the turmeric family.

In approximately 650 BCE, Ashurbanipal, king of Assyria, commissioned a research project to record information about cultivated herbs, plants, and spices. Recorded on thousands of clay tablets, data about approximately 250 plants was collected, among them turmeric. It was mentioned not only as a culinary spice, but as a plant used in brewing, dyeing, and medicine.

Theophrastus (born c. 372 BCE), a student of Aristotle, wrote about not only philosophy but zoology and botany. Living in the time of Alexander the Great's journey to India, he documented turmeric as one of the exotic plants brought back to Greece from that epic voyage. He was the first to group turmeric, as a species, together with ginger and cardamom as possible relatives. Marco Polo reported seeing turmeric grown in India for use as a fabric dye.

Although we might think of turmeric today as merely an exotic Asian spice associated with curry, it has a wide world footprint when one looks for its linguistic presence:

Cuncuma – Sanskrit
Turmeryte – Middle English; 1st recorded example 15th century
Haldi – Hindi (Northern India)
Manjal – Hindi (Southern India)
Manjano - Swahili
Ughe – Vietnamese
Khamin – Thai
Yu-jin/Jiang huang ("yellow ginger") – Chinese
Besar/Haledo – Nepali
Olena – Hawaiian
Kurkum – Hebrew and Arabic

This final root word, as pointed out by Gary Paul Nabhan in *Cumin, Camels and Caravans: A Spice Odyssey*, connects turmeric with the role of Jewish merchants who expanded the spice trade throughout Europe and Africa. According to Nabhan, derivatives of the Hebrew root word for turmeric turn up in "Yiddish, Greek, Italian, Bulgarian, Russian, Ukrainian, Korean, Finnish, Norwegian, German, Estonian, Czech, Croatian, Dutch, Breton, Catalan, Spanish and even Korean" (p. 38).

A cousin of ginger, cardamom, and galangal in the Zingiberaceae family, turmeric is a stately perennial plant with elegant elliptical leaves and yellow flowers, growing up to three feet tall. It's best harvested when the plant has delivered the maximum amount of nutrients to the rhizome, at six months of growth or later. Not only the rhizome but the leaves are used in cooking and traditional medicine. The aromatic leaves wrap cooked fish in Indonesia; in India the dried and ground root gives curry blends and dyed fabric its intensely saturated yellow hue. The sacred thread that is tied around the bride's neck by the bridegroom in Hindu weddings is dipped in turmeric paste. Monks' robes are still traditionally dyed with it to signal their vocation.

Yellow, in Hinduism, is not only a solar emblem but a symbol of purity, joy, wisdom, and renewal, associated with the garments worn by major deities. Although saffron also yields an intense (and somewhat more orange) fabric dye, turmeric is far cheaper and easier to produce as a dyestuff. Sometimes called "poor man's saffron," or "Indian saffron," deceptively marketed as the more expensive spice itself, turmeric was implicated in grocery fraud early in its history.

Without a mordant, turmeric acts as a "fugitive" dye, meaning it will fade fairly rapidly with exposure to sunlight and laundering. Since it is a food, turmeric solution is harmless to submerge your hands in when dyeing fiber or fabric, although it will stain your hands and nails with repeated exposure. Fresh turmeric roots will yield a more saturated golden color than dried turmeric. With an iron mordant, turmeric creates a woodsy green dye. Turmeric gained a strong foothold once it reached Africa, in many regions more as a dye than as a food.

Medicinally, turmeric is anti-inflammatory, stimulant, carminative, antiparasitic, antiseptic, antifungal, antioxidant, and possesses anticoagulant properties. It has been used in traditional medicine to treat ailments of the liver and gallbladder, as it aids bile flow and elimination. The essential oil or paste of the root is used externally for arthritis, rheumatism, skin rashes, and wound healing.

Paracelsus, the 16th century alchemist and physician, identified turmeric as a liver and gallbladder aid based on its color, since bile is yellow. In this case, as we can now confirm, his "doctrine of signatures" theory was actually correct.

In Thailand turmeric is used to neutralize cobra venom, and in China it has been used to treat epilepsy. In Hawaiian folk magic traditions, it is used with salt for rituals of purification and protection. In the ancient Indian scripts known as the Vedas, from which the system of Ayurvedic healthcare is drawn, turmeric is considered to be a warming and strengthening spice, beneficial to all three human physical profiles (*doshas*). The Mundas, an indigenous tribe of India, were named in the early Vedic literature as *nishada* (turmeric eaters).

It is one of the powerhouse herbs—useful inside and out.

Turmeric roots are knobby and thin-skinned, similar to the rhizomes of ginger. Thinner and smaller than ginger, about finger-sized, turmeric root has a distinct golden hue to its skin, and vibrant golden pith. Peeled, it can be eaten raw, cooked, or dried to be ground into the intensely yellow powder sold in tempting heaps in spice markets throughout the world.

Its flavor is sharp-sweet and more gingery when raw or cooked fresh, deepening into more bitter, nutty, woody notes when dried. Like ginger, ideal turmeric roots at the market are plump, unwrinkled, and firm. They will keep up to two weeks in the refrigerator and may also be frozen, although some softening of the root will result. Being a fairly weatherproof rhizome, it is easy to see how quickly turmeric could have been carried successfully far from Southeast Asia, as the roots travel well and can be planted and cultivated with fair tolerance even in more northerly climates.

Curcuma longa. Drakestein, H.A. van, *Hortus Indicus Malabaricus*, 1692. *plantillustrations.org*

The spice trade having fluctuated throughout history, it is difficult to pin down the "when" of a spice's arrival at a particular place and time, given that written records of food history often don't exist. We know that spice use varied widely throughout history depending on local economies, trade routes, and fashion. It is true that spices were typically more accessible to the wealthy, used as a status symbol. But it's a mistake to think that spices such as turmeric were used strictly as preservatives, or as a disguise for spoiled meat (a common misconception about spices in foods, especially in the medieval period).

Turmeric and other spices do indeed act as preservatives, but there are much easier and cheaper ways to preserve food which were used by our ancestors, even in hot climates—salting, sun-drying, or pickling. Volatile spices such as turmeric burn easily and are best activated by adding them to foods at the end of cooking, so that their essential oils and aromatic qualities are not destroyed by heat or oxidation. However, it must be noted that turmeric's primary beneficial chemical, curcumin, is fat soluble, and thus should be cooked with a substance (for example, coconut oil), that will allow it to become bioavailable when consumed. It is also synergized by the piperine in black pepper, which is why commercial vitamin supplements often contain the two combined.

Spices not only rise and fall in availability depending on the world's economy, but they also fall in and out of fashion and style. Spices speak to a culture's concepts of good taste and civilized living. We can't imagine not having curry powder in our own pantries today. But "curry," which is a loaded word with many meanings across time, was a turmeric-rich player in the entire history of the British occupation of India; first reviled as part of a peasant's spice blend, then exalted, and finally a constant in the air outside every curry shop in Britain.

Looking back in time, the cuisine of the medieval period in Europe was indeed laden with sweet, sour, and spicy flavors, employing many spices we still use today, including turmeric.

Then, economies, empires, and tastes shifted. The Portuguese, Dutch, and the British became locked in conflicts for control of the spice routes from Asia to Europe in the 17th century; eventually the British achieved dominion by installing the East India Company as an occupying force in the subcontinent. By the 18th century, Continental food preferences had taken a milder turn towards French cuisine, with blander seasonings; excess "spice" was seen as vulgar, or at the least unhealthful. Newer, more trendy commodities such as coffee, tea, and cocoa were dominating global markets.

Yet in early America, wealthy colonists were eagerly receiving their imported spices from overseas, via England or the Caribbean. In 1809 India Wharf was built in Boston to berth spice ships arriving from Calcutta, helping make turmeric-laced curries a common offering in the city's harborside taverns. Spices, it seems, never truly go out of style.

Eventually, British colonial domination in India fanned an absolute craze for the new, exotic and more pungent flavors produced by Asian spices, including turmeric. By the time Queen Victoria became Empress of India in 1877, a full-blown rage for all things Indian—food, décor, ornaments, art, textiles—was aflame in Britain, and curry was central within that craze. Yet at the same time, the new elite British expatriates, living overseas in India, were beginning to look down on native cuisine, falling back to un-spicy British and French styles of cooking. Curry was seen as army-barracks food, stodge for laborers. Spicy food was not what polite society ate back home. Or so they thought. Because curry, and with it, turmeric, was by then firmly embedded in cuisine not only in Britain, but across the globe.

By the 1950's, attitudes on the Continent toward immigrants and their native cuisines had turned yet again, and curry, or the smell of its pungent spices, was associated with poverty and lower class cuisine. Yet curry shops, and with them plenty of turmeric, were thronged, and still are today.

We don't tend to pick turmeric out and look at it alone, aside from its role in curry powders. But as an herb, turmeric holds its own in the medicinal, culinary and cosmetic arenas.

Turmeric continues to flourish … and be carried far afield. As it should be!

References

Alford, Jeremy and Duguid, Naomi. *Hot Sour Salty Sweet: A Culinary Journey Through Southeast Asia.* Workman Publishing Company, Inc., 2000.

_____. *Mangoes and Curry Leaves: Culinary Travels Through The Great Subcontinent.* Workman Publishing Company, Inc., 2005.

Balch, James F., M.D. and Stengler, Mark, M.D. *Prescription For Natural Cures.* John Wiley & Sons, Inc., 2004.

Bremness, Lesley. *Herbs.* DK Publishing, Inc., 1994.

Bsisu, May S. *The Arab Table: Recipes and Culinary Traditions.* HarperCollins Publishers, 2005.

Castleman, Michael. *The Healing Herbs.* Rodale Press, 1991.

Cunningham, Scott. *Cunningham's Encyclopedia of Magical Herbs.* Llewellyn Worldwide, Ltd.: 1985.

Duerr, Sasha. *The Handbook of Natural Plant Dyes.* Timber Press, Inc., 2010.

Duke, James A., Ph.D. *A Field Guide To Medicinal Plants: Eastern and Central North America.* Rodale Press, 1987.

_____. *The Green Pharmacy.* Rodale Press, 1997.

Fougère, Barbara, BVSc. *The Pet Lover's Guide to Natural Healing for Cats & Dogs.* Elsevier Saunders, 2006.

Gerard, John. *The Herball or Generall Historie of Plantes.* London, United Kingdom: John Norton, 1597.

Green, Aliza. *Field Guide To Herbs And Spices.* Quirk Books, 2006.

Grieve, Mrs. Maud. *A Modern Herbal In Two Volumes*; Vol. II: I-Z. Dover Publications, 1971.

Hutton, Wendy. *Green Mangoes and Lemon Grass.* Singapore: Periplus Editions, 2004.

Illes, Judika. *The Encyclopedia of 5,000 Spells.* HarperCollins, 2008.

Morgan, Diane. *Roots.* Chronicle Books LLC, 2012.

Nabhan, Gary Paul. *Cumin, Camels and Caravans: A Spice Odyssey.* University of California Press, 2014.

Neal, Bill. *Gardener's Latin.* Algonquin Books, 1992.

Personal notes, Proceedings of the International Herb Symposium, Norton, MA, 2000-2013.

Poth, Susanne, and Sauer, Gina. *The Spice Lilies: Eastern Secrets to Healing with Ginger, Turmeric, Cardamom and Galangal.* Healing Arts Press, 2000.

Rose, Jeanne. *375 Essential Oils and Hydrosols.* Frog, Ltd., 1999.

Sahni, Julie. *Classic Indian Cooking.* William Morrow and Company, Inc., 1980.

Sukhadwala, Sejal. *The Philosophy of Curry.* The British Library, 2022.

Tilford, Gregory L. and Wulff-Tilford, Mary. *All You Ever Wanted To Know About Herbs for Pets.* Bowtie Press, 1999.

Tiwari, Maya. *Ayurveda: A Life of Balance.* Healing Arts Press, 1995.

Wright, Clifford W. *A Mediterranean Feast.* William Morrow and Company, Inc., 1999.

Rosemary Roman Davis was raised in a family of herbalists and green thumbs, and maintains a messy but vibrant organic garden in upstate New York. One of her first paid jobs as a high school student was office assistant at the Herb Society of America, long ago when its headquarters were located in Concord, MA. When not finding new excuses to avoid weeding, and planning for the next big endeavor—beekeeping—she is a licensed massage therapist and Reiki Master. She has also been an adult education teacher for over fifteen years, offering food folklore classes and many hands-on workshops including soapmaking, cheesemaking and papermaking.

Rosemary Davis: "Spices speak to a culture's concepts of good taste and civilized living." *Susan Belsinger*

Turmeric root harvest. *Helen Lowe Metzman*

Growing, Using, and Honoring Turmeric

Jane Hawley Stevens

Research on an herb not typically in my repertoire of growing and integrating it into my everyday kitchen pharmacy is a fun and interesting challenge. Sure, I use turmeric, but it was not my go-to herb. The quest for an engaging, informational, and insightful article for IHA became a rare opportunity to get to share my experiences learning about and growing turmeric. I am at the library of United Plant Savers, UPS, in Rutland, Ohio. They recently acquired four libraries of industry icons: Jim Duke, Stephen Harrod Buhner, John Staba, and David Winston. I am doing my research on turmeric using this extensive library; I feel like it is the best herb library on the planet under one roof!

Studying turmeric has left me feeling like I do after a deep dive into many herbal qualities. It does everything but scratch your back! I say this lovingly of lemon balm, *Melissa officinalis,* sage, *Salvia officinalis,* and yarrow, *Achillea millifolium,* to name a few examples.

Turmeric, *Curcuma longa*, has been used as a spice, medicine, coloring, and in rituals since before Dioscorides, and was mentioned as far back as 600 BC. It is native to India and Southeast Asia.

The intense yellow pigment holds the active ingredients and integrates easily into body systems through many biochemical pathways. Current studies have shown that the piperene from black pepper aids in the body's absorption of turmeric's constituents. The therapeutic qualities of turmeric include anticancer and chemoprotective, anti-inflammatory, antioxidant, antimicrobial, improves cardio-vascular function, inhibits carcinogens and tumor promotion, is tissue protective and neuroprotective. This would make it useful for treating arthritis, inflammation of all kinds, after surgery, for dental care, sprains, bruises, and inflammatory bowel conditions. It has been noted to help with psoriasis as well. Plus, it makes your food pretty, with its deep golden yellow color.

Turmeric tea is a wise choice for its anti-inflammatory and anti-cancer benefits. Turmeric has been proven to match the effects of cortisone shots in scientific studies (Bone and Mills, 2013). A laboratory study found that joint pain from rheumatoid arthritis was reduced by 48% on day three and an additional 45% on day 23 (Funk, et al.,2006). Turmeric was found to reduce cataracts in laboratory rats with "significantly less damage than in the control animals" (Padmaja, 2004).

Additional research is showing that there is reason to believe that this simple herb could help prevent Alzheimer's disease. Curcumin can enter the brain, bind to plaque, and reduce plaque size by 30 percent (Cole, et al., 2007).

The anti-cancer effects of turmeric on breast, lung, liver, oral, and gastric cancers have been studied; it has been found to have antitumor activity and can be considered a cancer prevention herb. Turmeric can inhibit tumors by blocking the activation of carcinogens or by stimulating detoxification. The anti-inflammatory effect alone signals cells to stop cancer cells' bad behavior, like a stressed 1950s mother reprimanding their children, "Stop NOW!" Turmeric can inhibit cancer cell proliferation and survival.

To underscore the value of this herb, remember it is easy to ingest both as tea or in cooking, and it gets absorbed into the body very easily. A study of laboratory rats that ingested turmeric as 1 percent of their diet and then were exposed to fumigated fuel smoke showed that there was a reduction in the formation of dangerous benzopyrene, thus reducing DNA damage (Shalini, 1990).

Turmeric, endemic to India, is esteemed for its protective nature in the Hindu religion, where it is incorporated into many rituals. It is considered protective, warding off evil spirits, and as a conduit of blessings from Ganesha and Gauri. I often wonder if cultures found a correlation or energy around a plant, knowing the virtues were many, then considered it sacred, holding a life force understood before science could prove it. Heart disease is less prevalent in regions where turmeric use is common, and I can see why it could be regarded as a blessing.

Often, when I study the ritual uses of herbs, the high esteem in which these plants are held makes sense; for they promote good health and improved quality and enjoyment of life. Traditional in India, turmeric is used as a stomach relaxer, tonic, and blood purifier. It is a remedy for poor digestion, fevers, skin conditions, liver disorders; and can be externally applied for skin infections, cancers, sprains, arthritis, hemorrhoids, and eczema, as well as for wound healing. In some cases, Eastern and Western traditions using turmeric overlap, for example in the treatment of aches, sprains, and contusions

I became familiar with Eastern turmeric rituals last month during my daughter's Hindu wedding at our farm. The women of the family were excited to decorate the altar or mandir with the turmeric plants that I grew. The night before the wedding, the bride and groom typically enter a Haldi ritual of loved ones washing them with a turmeric paste or infusion to protect them from evil. The vibrant yellow is auspicious, evoking purity, good fortune, happiness, protection, love, and good energy.

Turmeric's Uses in Ritual

Purification: Turmeric is traditionally used to purify the body and soul, opening up space for new beginnings.

Prosperity: The yellow color of turmeric symbolizes wealth, prosperity, and happiness.

Protection: Turmeric paste is applied as a protective shield, warding off negative spirits.

Auspiciousness: Turmeric is considered sacred and is used to invoke blessings in rituals of new beginnings.

Sacred Offerings: Turmeric is made into a paste with sandalwood and is offered to the deities during holy days or rituals.

Protection: Turmeric paste is applied to household doorframes as protection—like using rue or St. John's wort in Europe, white sage in Southwest indigenous cultures, and tulsi, also in India.

Dye for Religious Garments: The natural dye properties color the saffron-colored robes worn by Hindu priests.

Festivals and Rituals: Turmeric symbolizes a bountiful harvest and triumph of good over evil.

Although turmeric is inexpensive in bulk, I would encourage anyone to grow some in a pot or garden spot. It is so easy to control, not prone to weeds, and grows in a tight clump with large leaves, so it can fit in a tight spot, pot, or fill a square foot of space in the garden. Commercially purchased turmeric has been shown to contain lead, so it is best to find organically grown rhizomes, (especially for consumption). By growing your own, you can control the habitat, nutrients, and give it any special touches you may have developed in your gardening practices. Turmeric is a fun plant to grow and watch, as the large leaves develop and the knobby rhizomes increase in diameter.

According to Dr. James Duke, two of the best turmeric varieties are Deshi and Patani, each named for the regions of India from which they originate. Patani is thought to have better color and flavor. The local Indian variety Chinna Nadan is said to grow more vigorously, have a sweeter aroma, a deep golden-yellow color, and high curcumin content, which is naturally more stable, bioavailable, and beneficial (www.goodness-farm.com).

To produce a quantity of turmeric rhizomes, I would plant it in a raised bed.

One season of growing turmeric from rhizome in Wisconsin. *Jane Hawley Stevens*

I plant all Mediterranean crops and root crops in raised beds or hills set in place with a tractor and a hiller/modified disk setup. This offers perfect drainage for these crops such as sage, rosemary, lavender, thyme that prefer soil moist, but never wet, and for root crops that are easier to harvest if they have been grown in loose soil, provided by hilling.

In Southern Asia and India, turmeric is grown in fertile soils with good drainage. Rhizomes are placed about 1.5 feet apart in May or June, similar to what we would do here in zone 4. Some species of *Curcuma* are grown in India at higher altitudes, including some of the lower Himalayan ranges, but *C. longa* is grown near Bombay, Madras, and Bengal. Turmeric cultivated in the hills is said to have better quality than that raised in the hotter plains of India. This is a plus for us living in more temperate zones.

Manure is added to the soil when the soil is being worked. Organic standards in America require that there be 100 days between planting and harvesting

Two-year-old potted turmeric, wintered over in the basement, yielded almost 2 pounds of rhizome*s. Jane Hawley Stevens*

when using aged manure. Keeping the plants moist, but not wet, will ensure progressive growth. A raised bed with compost added will ensure good drainage in saturated times.

Cultivation

The plant needs hot and moist conditions, similar to the signature of arthritis and inflammation. A liberal water supply will help turmeric thrive in most soil types, as long as the soil is loose. Gravelly, stony, or clay soils are not suitable.

These are the recommendations from the *Dictionary of the Economic Products of India:*

Till soil to one foot deep

Spread manure and till 3 more times.

Make ridges and set rhizomes each with 1 to 2 buds, 3 inches deep, 12 to 15 inches apart.

Although these recommendations suggest 12-inch spacing, studies in Ceylon showed that plants spaced 6- x 6-inches apart generated more rhizomes than those spaced 12- x 12-inches apart. Crops are harvested after 9 to 10 months of growing. Try both spacing methods in your garden to determine what is right for you.

Curing: Bulbous and finger-shaped roots are separated, and long fingers are broken into pieces. This loosens the soil to be brushed off. Curing in India is done by cooking the rhizomes in water with a couple of leaves. Cow dung is said to intensify the color. I think mine is yellow enough for me. (Another reason to grow your own if that sounds unappealing). The remaining bits that fall off the plants in cleaning are used to fertilize the paddy fields. I appreciate this as a giving back to the land, incorporating a sense of gratitude for the harvest. Sometimes color is enhanced by putting some tamarind rind in the cooking water, which also rids the rhizomes of pests.

To implement my gardening practices from *Gardening by the Moon and Zodiac,* I would plan the hilling, which is best done before the Full Moon, to be done between the New and Full Moon. This is when the soil is lighter and easier to shape into hills. I would plant turmeric, a root crop, in the third quarter, just past the Full Moon. Coastal dwellers know that the tide is highest at the Full Moon. Right after that, the tide decreases and so does the water table below the soil surface, even if you are not near the ocean. This timing encourages healthy and more robust root growth, as the water table lowers. I have seen this phenomenon in action with potatoes and carrots! To add another dimension of planetary influence, I would check the almanacs or my *Gardening by the Moon* calendar for the influence of an Earth Sign, which rules root crops. Look for the Moon in Taurus, Virgo, or Capricorn, the Earth Signs, for an extra astrological boost.

Jupiter is the ruling planet of turmeric according to Vedic, or Indian, astrology. Jupiter favors expansion (I think of the rhizomes here) and represents wisdom, knowledge, blessings, abundance, and good fortune.

My horticulture mentor, Chris Hopka, gave me a piece of turmeric that he had stored in his basement over the winter, and a potted turmeric plant that was still leafy from being in his greenhouse the prior year. In my zone 4, with a good growing season, both were grown in pots. The pieces of turmeric that were first started this season took a long time to sprout and yielded just 4.4 ounces. The potted turmeric, leafy and bold, yielded just over 2 pounds. I would recommend leaving turmeric in a pot over the winter if you would like to grow it the following year. You can let it go dormant in the winter in a cool, dark place, as you would geraniums. In the spring, you will have a more robust start than just-sprouting turmeric rhizomes.

From these potted rhizomes comes my first-hand account of Chris's daily use of turmeric tea. He grates about two tablespoons of fresh turmeric root into about one quart of water. Turmeric can be simmered fresh (or dried) for 5 to 10 minutes, then left to steep, for another 10 minutes to several hours. Chris has been growing greenhouses full of the most remarkable flowering potted plants you have ever seen for over five decades, with very few complaints of

aches and pains. I believe the support and actions of the turmeric tea keep him growing strong with joy. He makes his turmeric decoction with freshly grated turmeric every day, and he has definitely earned this privilege.

Holly's teapot, used exclusively for the turmeric tea that Chris makes for them daily. *Jane Hawley Stevens*

According to acupuncturist and herbalist, Laurel Redmon, this traditional amount—2 tablespoons—in food or tea, of turmeric daily is the best way to get proper results. I sometimes steep turmeric tea, then add more water to enjoy the next day as an overnight infusion.

Turmeric can be extracted in alcohol and used in tincture form, or used as a powder, adding a heaping teaspoon to any meal, beverage, or condiment twice daily for its benefits. No adverse effects have been reported, which, compared to over-the-counter anti-inflammatories, is a good choice for long-term use. Dried turmeric can be put into capsules to save some money. Be careful where you assemble these! My niece was on the crew team at the University of Michigan and wanted to try some turmeric, so I brought some powdered and dried herb and some gel caps. Since I wanted to be with everyone, I took a tray into the living room to work on this project. Something happened to tip the tray, spilling the dried turmeric on her couch! My only consolation was that she was a student and would be moving soon, leaving the forever yellow-stained couch behind.

Esteem and reverence are certainly deserving adjectives for this highly versatile and potent rhizome and herb, as borrowed from the Hindu tradition. Moving forward, I will be handling and utilizing this gift of Nature with more gratitude and admiration for its health-enhancing qualities, beauty, ease of cultivation, and all-around protective nature. So, let's grow turmeric!

Where to find dried turmeric in bulk:

Mountain Rose Herbs
Frontier Herbs
Monterey Bay
Starwest Botanicals

References

"Beyond Curcumin: Why the Whole Turmeric Profile Matters." www.goodness-farm.com. Accessed 10-22-25.

Bone, Kerry, and Mills, Simon. *Principles and Practice of Phytotherapy*. Churchstone Livingston, 2013. 900-919.

Cole GM, Teter B, Frautschy SA. *Adv Exp Med Biol*. 2007. 197-212.

Funk JL, Oyarzo, JN, et al. *J Nat Prod*. 2006. 351-355.

Mehra KS, Mikuni I, Gupta V, et al. *Tokai J Exp Clin Med.* 1984. 27-31.

Padmaja S, Raju TN. *Indian J Exp Biol.* 2004. 601-603.

Shalini VK, Srinivas L. *Mol Cell Biochem.* 1990. 21-30.

The Wealth of India, A Dictionary of Indian Raw Materials and Industrial Products, Vol 2. Delhi, 1950. 402-407

Watt, George. *Dictionary of the Economic Products of India*, Vol 2. Shahadra, Delhi, 1972. 659-669.

Jane Hawley Stevens plants, harvests, and creates herbal wellness for her brand, Four Elements Organic Herbals, from her 130-acre farm in Wisconsin. She and her husband, David, received the Organic Farmer of the Year award in 2020. Jane is a pioneer in organic farming and natural products communities and has been certified organic since 1989, specializing in herbs since graduating with a horticulture degree in the 80s.

Jane believes in cultivating Nature's wisdom with its beauty and rhythms, knowing it is up to all of us to contribute to our planet's health and sustainability.

She spends her time gardening, hiking, biking, or skiing to be surrounded by the beauty and awe that can only be experienced outdoors. You can find her at night, gazing at the stars and planets with reverence for the opportunity to be an advocate for Nature and all of its wonderment.

A pioneer of the organic farming movement and natural products industry, Jane inspires others through living her truth, bringing herbal wellness to the marketplace through her product line, Four Elements Organic Herbals, and teaching herbalism and organic farming methods throughout the country. Her recent book is *The Celestial Garden: Growing Herbs, Vegetables, and Flowers in Sync with the Moon and Zodiac.*

Jane Hawley Stevens
Four Elements Organic Herbals
PO Box 10
North Freedom WI 53951
608-522-4492

Harmonizing Health Through Nature's Beauty since 1987.

Turmeric
in
the
Kitchen

Fleshy, plump turmeric rhizomes can be grated to use fresh in recipes and are easy to slice into "coins." *Susan Belsinger*

Trending Turmeric

Susan Belsinger

Turmeric has steadily been building in popularity over recent years due to its amazing health attributes—especially its antioxidant and anti-inflammatory benefits. The health-giving properties are covered in the medicinal section of this book so I will not go on about that here. Rather, I shall talk about it more in a culinary vein.

I really first became acquainted with turmeric back in the 70s and wrote about that in my golden milk article (p. 145). Currently, that beverage is all the rage—and it is indeed a wonderful wellness beverage to drink before sleep.

In *Spice Health Heroes*, author Natasha MacAller calls turmeric *the master spice*, stating, "Some consider turmeric the most powerful spice in the pantry. Not only does this rhizome give curry dishes their distinctive, rich earthy flavor, but turmeric is quite possibly the oldest and most scientifically studied spice in the world." In medieval times, Ottoman traders brought turmeric to Europe, where it was used as an alternative to saffron, thus the monikers Indian saffron and false saffron. Globally, most of the turmeric is grown in India and there are two main kinds: the pungent, deep ochre-hued 'Alleppey' is the most esteemed of these rhizomes, while 'Madras' is brighter yellow in color and has a bit of sweetness to its taste.

There are some foods as well as seasonings that I know (although I am sure there are a vast number of Indian dishes and spice blends) which cannot be made without turmeric. The dried ground powder is essential to spice blends like curry powder, *ras-el-hanout*, and *garam masala*, as well as condiments such as American yellow mustard, English piccalilli and pickles of all sorts.

The inimitable flavor of turmeric is at first earthy with musky, woody and bitter notes and some pungency, which is due to the flavor compounds tumerone and ar-tumerone. Eleanor Ford, author of *A Whisper of Cardamom* (I have attended her Smithsonian webinars—one in particular on turmeric—I

Here's the holy turmeric trio for getting that curcumin absorbed into the body: fresh or ground turmeric rhizome, black peppercorns and fat (any healthy oil or butter). *Susan Belsinger*

would say she is a spice expert) describes: "Turmeric's earthiness serves to bind other flavors together and give depth" and further "To keep turmeric's vibrancy, store away from light and use alongside an acid such as lemon juice to make the color pop."

I use both the fresh and dried ground rhizome in recipes—I love the flavor of the fresh in recipes as it has more zest and stronger flavor—although I use the ground often also. Of course, in my spice blends, I use the ground. I use fresh grated when I have it and where I want it to really brighten a dish—especially in the following turmeric shots and sauerkraut recipes.

I find that turmeric stored in plastic often gets wet and molds, so I tend to keep my fresh rhizomes in a brown paper bag on the door of the refrigerator. Inevitably if left too long it will dry up. When I have excess fresh rhizomes, I break them into fingers and put them into small, tightly sealed freezer containers and freeze them. When needed, I take them from the freezer and chop or grate them and they work quite well, although they are a little watery. Alternatively, grate the rhizomes and add a bit of coconut or grapeseed oil to just barely moisten and a few grinds of black pepper and freeze in small containers; spoon out as needed.

For the best absorption of the curcumin in turmeric, one needs to add just a little bit of freshly ground black pepper into the same dish (not the pre-ground pepper which has lost much of its piperine), and a little bit of fat also helps with the absorption.

As I write this, I look at my hands which are stained yellow from curcumin. It is evident that I have been testing turmeric recipes this week. Turmeric

stains hands, clothes (my apron is pretty much covered in multi-colored bright yellow blotches), cutting boards, food processors, plastic containers as well as kitchen counters and appliances! So be aware and take precautions—it doesn't wash off—though it may eventually wear off.

Easy to make and quite tasty to drink—it doesn't last long around our house!
Susan Belsinger

Turmeric Shots

Turmeric shots are very popular these days and are available at groceries, health food stores, smoothie and juice bars; however they are very easy to make at home and will be much fresher, not to mention you can use whatever juices you like best. These little power shooters build your immune system and boost your energy. I looked at a lot of recipes online and drank quite a few commercial ones that are available and decided I like mine made in my own kitchen best. I have adapted my own version from the following two recipes: https://turmericlife.com/blogs/news/turmeric-citrus-wellness-shot-recipe-by-dr-doug *and* https://www.verywellhealth.com/turmeric-shots-8784927.

The boiling water helps to dissolve the oil and honey and "cooks"' the turmeric. Adding the fat and black pepper helps the body to better absorb the curcumin in the turmeric. Use fresh-squeezed juices—not from concentrate. This is a strong-flavored potion; you might want to use the lesser amount of turmeric and ginger at first—or just go for the gusto!

Makes about 1 1/14 cups; shot glass-size is a serving

About 1 1/2 to 2 tablespoons freshly grated turmeric root
About 1 tablespoon local honey or pure maple syrup
Scant 1/2 teaspoon coconut oil
3 tablespoons boiling water
1 cup fresh-squeezed orange or apple cider/juice
About 1 1/2 tablespoons fresh-squeezed lemon juice
About 1 1/2 to 2 tablespoons freshly grated gingerroot
Few grinds of black pepper
Coconut water, optional

In a measuring cup, combine the turmeric root, honey and coconut oil. Pour the boiling water into the cup and stir well to dissolve the honey and oil. Cool to room temperature.

In a larger measuring cup, combine the orange and lemon juice and stir in the gingerroot. Pour the turmeric mixture and the orange juice mixture into a blender and add a few grinds of black pepper. Blend for 20 to 30 seconds until well combined.

Let stand for 5 to 10 minutes and strain the beverage through a strainer. Serve immediately or refrigerate for up to a few days. If you'd like it further diluted, add a little coconut water. Sip slowly; hold in your mouth for a few seconds before swallowing so it mixes with your saliva.

Golden Glow Sauerkraut

This sauerkraut is bright yellow due to using turmeric. It is a fairly simple, basic sauerkraut recipe with creative possibilities to follow. Salt should be non-iodized; I prefer Celtic sea salt. I cut back on the salt and use an equal amount of seaweed for saltiness and flavor. You can use any sea vegetable like dulse, kombu, wakame, hijiki, arame, even nori—just be sure to cut it into small pieces (I generally use scissors). If you don't use the seaweed, you will probably have to add a bit more salt. Pretty much anything goes when making sauerkraut—you can vary ingredients for flavor—add herbs and spices or other vegetables. Other roots like turnip or parsnip can be used in place of the daikon. Probably my best advice is not to add too many ingredients; keep it simple.

Makes about 1 to 1 1/2 quarts

1 small- to medium-size head cabbage; remove a few outer leaves and reserve
1 medium sweet or yellow onion
2 medium-size carrots, coarsely grated
1 medium daikon radish, coarsely grated
2 or 3 cloves slivered garlic
About 1 tablespoon sea salt (non-iodized)
About 1 tablespoon slivered seaweed, optional
2 to 3 tablespoons fresh grated turmeric
1 generous tablespoon fresh grated ginger
1/2 teaspoon each: medium ground caraway and coriander seeds

Tools needed: 1 gallon glass jar, 1 gallon freezer, zip-close bag or air-lock fermentation lid, big bowl, potato masher or large pestle, knife, cutting board. Slice, shred and/or chop your cabbage and onion fairly fine. You can use a kraut slicer if you have one, but it's not necessary. Cut the onion in half lengthwise, cut the halves in half crosswise and thinly slice. In a big bowl, toss the cabbage, onion, carrots, daikon and garlic to mix the vegetables. Sprinkle with 1 tablespoon of the salt and the pieces of seaweed and mix well. Knead with your hands to start the process, allowing the cabbage to give off juice. Pound with the potato masher or pestle to release more liquid from the vegetables.

Top, just mixed kraut; bottom, Golden Glow Sauerkraut after fermentation. *Susan Belsinger*

Taste for salt and add a bit more as needed. When the kraut is juicy, put it into a very clean gallon jar. If the kraut is not giving off enough juice, allow it to sit for a while (30 to 60 minutes) and repeat the kneading process.

Pack the cabbage into the jar and press very firmly to get rid of all air bubbles and to pack so tightly that the juice rises above it. Once the jar is firmly packed with all of the cabbage, cover the packed cabbage with a few whole leaves and press down firmly.

If you don't have a fermentation lid, put a gallon zip-close bag in the top of the jar and add about a cup of cold water; put your hand inside the bag and press down firmly yet carefully to seal the bag all around the edges and top of the cabbage to remove all of the air and make sure that the cabbage is submerged under the juice. Once you are satisfied that you have sealed the top, add another cup or so of water to weight the bag and carefully press out excess air, then seal the bag closed.

Or, use a fermentation air-lock type lid. Leave the jar on the counter, at room temperature, dry and out of the sun for 1 to 2 weeks. After about 5 to 7 days, remove the fermentation lid or pull the bag off the jar, pour the water out of the bag, and taste your kraut. The length of time for fermentation really does vary. In hot weather my kraut is often ready in 5 days. In cooler weather, it can easily ferment for 2 weeks. If you are happy with the taste then your fermentation is complete—if you want it to ferment more, just put the lid back on or put the bag back in, resealing as described above and let it go another few days. Once fermented, transfer the kraut into smaller jars and store it in the fridge. Eat the kraut fresh; it is best eaten in the first few months, though it will keep in fridge for up to a year. You can add a very wide variety of ingredients to kraut. Experiment and enjoy!

creative possibilities

▶ Add seaweed flakes or minced seaweed and use less salt

▶ Use leek in place of onion; substitute other leafy greens (like kale) for cabbage

▶ Add spicy ingredients like horseradish, chile peppers or grated gingerroot

▶ Add herbs like dill, fennel, parsley, bay leaves

▶ Add spices like caraway, celery seed, coriander and cumin seed, paprika and turmeric

Tofu Spread with Jalapeño & Turmeric

This recipe is adapted from a recipe from <u>Vegetarian Cooking for Everyone</u> by Deborah Madison. If you don't like it spicy, omit the chile pepper. It is delicious as a sandwich spread or served on bagels, pitas, crackers or crudites.

Makes about 3 cups

10-ounce package firm tofu
1/4 cup finely diced red bell pepper
1/4 cup finely diced onion
1 small to medium carrot, grated
1 jalapeño or serrano, stemmed, seeded, and diced
1 or 2 large cloves garlic, pressed
2 tablespoons fresh minced parsley
1/4 cup + 1 tablespoon mayonnaise
1 tablespoon Dijon-style mustard
1 teaspoon ground, dried turmeric or 1 tablespoon fresh grated turmeric
1/2 teaspoon curry powder
1/4 teaspoon Hungarian paprika
1/4 teaspoon smoked paprika, optional
1/2 teaspoon salt, or to taste
Freshly ground pepper
3 to 5 dashes Angostura bitters
1 to 2 tablespoons sweet or sour pickle juice, or 1 tablespoon vinegar, optional

Drain the tofu in a colander and press the excess liquid from it. Transfer it to the bowl of a food processor and add the rest of the ingredients. Pulse to blend and break the veggies into smaller pieces, stopping once or twice to scrape down the sides. It shouldn't be a total puree; it should have some crunchy pieces for texture. It will be a crumbly paste; taste to see if it needs more seasoning, mustard or mayonnaise.

It tastes better after it stands for a while and flavors meld. Transfer to a container with a tight-fitting lid and refrigerate for at least an hour before serving. Taste for seasoning and adjust if needed. Let stand at room temperature for about 10 or 15 minutes before serving so it isn't icy cold.

Making your own mustards allows for a multitude of fun flavorings—the more you do it, the better it gets. *Susan Belsinger*

Mustard Musings

Susan Belsinger

Used by the Greeks and Romans, and mentioned numerous times in the Bible, mustard has been used for almost two thousand years, both culinarily and medicinally. Recipes for mustard preparations have been found written in the first century A.D. It is believed that the word mustard and the French *moutarde* comes from the Latin *mustum ardens* which means "burning must," a rather appropriate description. The ground mustard seeds were mixed with grape must (freshly pressed, unfermented juice) to make mustard in ancient times, similar to our prepared mustard of today. France is famous for combining mustard with vinegar, and Dijon exports its popular mustard throughout the world.

The two mustards seen most often throughout the world are the creamy pale Dijon-style and the darker Bordeaux. Dijon-style is light in color because the seed coat is removed, then it is combined with verjuice (sour, unripe juice) and ground to a very fine paste. It has a strong hot taste that is slightly salty and not at all sweet; no herbs are added. The Bordeaux-style is dark because it has not had the seed coat removed, it contains lots of tarragon, and sometimes other herbs or spices; and it is sweet and sour from the addition of sugar and vinegar.

German mustard can range from mild to hot and sweet to savory. The most common is dark mustard with a balance of vinegar and sugar, sometimes with the addition of herbs or spice, designed to go with their sausages. Chinese mustard is made from brown or black mustard seeds; it is sometimes called Asian mustard. It is usually the hottest of all prepared mustards so use it sparingly. It is commonly served with eggrolls. Prepared mustards can be stored in a cool dark place for up to 2 years, if unopened. Once opened, the mustard must be refrigerated.

Another universally popular type of prepared mustard is the bright yellow American-style one that we see most often in the U.S. The first recorded addition of turmeric to mustard is credited to George T. French, of the R.T.

French Company. In 1904, his sons, George and Francis introduced this bright yellow mustard at the St. Louis World's Fair and called it French's Classic Yellow Mustard and served it over hot dogs. It was first sold in a glass bottle with a screw-top lid.

This mustard is as American as apple pie and accompanies practically every hotdog eaten in the U.S. It is now found globally—however it is not one that I prefer as an adult—though I have been known to consume it with a salty soft pretzel every now and then.

It is made from yellow mustard seeds which are less pungent than the darker varieties. It has quite a bit of ground turmeric added which gives it its bright yellow color, and it also has vinegar and sugar added. An old-fashioned cookout would not be complete without this mustard to accompany hamburgers and hotdogs.

When I was a child, mustard was that bright yellow stuff in a jar that was always on the picnic table; sometimes it was in a yellow plastic squeeze bottle. It was striped on your hotdog along with ketchup. It was the only thing on your corned beef sandwich besides the rye bread. It was used to doctor up canned baked beans along with ketchup, onions, and brown sugar.

This turmeric-laden condiment is known round the world. *Susan Belsinger*

It was in my grandmother's deviled eggs. Any recipe that has devil in the title (i.e., Deviled Eggs, Deviled Crab, Deviled Ham) generally means that it has mustard in it. It became "deviled" because of the hotness the mustard added.

As I was growing up my mother used to make our ham, bologna, and cheese sandwiches by spreading mayonnaise on one slice of bread and mustard on the other slice of bread. This is a flavor that will be ingrained in my taste memory forever. A cheese sandwich just doesn't taste right unless the balance is there. As I grew up, I changed this formula just a bit by using Dijon-style mustard in place of the American-style that I grew up eating. Whenever I go camping or on a road trip with a cooler, I mix a jar of mustard and mayonnaise together for convenience. This combination is also wonderful on *pommes frites*. It is a cholesterol overload, but the first time I tasted French fried potatoes with mustard mayonnaise from a street vendor in Paris I was hooked. They were just as delicious in Amsterdam; they eat French fries all over Europe in this fashion—not with ketchup.

In this mustard recipe following, I combine a sort of French-style mustard with classic American additions of turmeric and honey—it is savory and sweet—the best of both worlds.

Golden Garlic Honey Mustard with Turmeric

This a simple, really basic mustard, that can be varied by using different vinegars, adding herbs or horseradish, or using maple syrup in place of the honey. It should be prepared in advance so the pungency has a chance to mellow as it is quite spicy (nearly inedible—think mustard gas) when first made. It is more wholesome and not as smooth as French's American-style yellow mustard, since that goes through a cooking process.

Makes a generous 3/4 cup

3/4 cup mustard powder, or freshly ground seed
1/4 cup + 1 tablespoon water
1/4 cup tarragon or white wine vinegar
1 tablespoon honey
1/4 teaspoon salt
1 teaspoon ground turmeric
1 clove garlic, pressed or minced fine

Blend the mustard with the water in a bowl with a small whisk and let it stand for 10 to 15 minutes. (This is done first to reduce bitterness—if vinegar is added at the beginning, the mustard tastes bitter.) The mustard will absorb the liquid as it stands. Add the vinegar, honey, salt, turmeric, and garlic and blend well. Add a little more water or vinegar if necessary to bring the mustard to a spreading consistency.

Pack into jars and keep refrigerated until ready to use. The mustard is very hot when first mixed, and mellows with age. When refrigerated, the mellowing process slows to nearly a stop. For a spicy, but not overwhelming mustard, store unopened, at room temperature for 4 to 6 weeks, and then place it in the refrigerator. Once opened, the mustard should be kept in the refrigerator.

Mustards are very pungent for the first 4 to 6 weeks; after 8 weeks they tend to lose their fire somewhat. Taste before using, and use accordingly since they can be quite pungent.

The golden glow of a fresh turmeric root provides the cook with flavor and color as well as many health-giving benefits. *Susan Belsinger*

Belsinger, Susan. *the perfect bite: focus on flavor*. Balboa Press, 2022.

_____. "Seeds of Desire", *Herb Companion,* September 1999, pages 25-31.

_____. https://courses.herbsociety.org/courses/take/gathering-and-preserving-the-herbal-bounty/lessons/35199721-herbal-mustards. Accessed 8/5/25.

Farrimond, Stuart, Dr. *The Science of Spice*. Dorling Kindersley, 2018.

Ford, Eleanor. *A Whisper of Cardamom*. Apollo, 2024.

https://topsecretrecipes.com/frenchs-classic-yellow-mustard-copycat-recipe.html. Accessed 8/5/25.

https://www.mccormick.com/pages/frenchs-story, Accessed 8//5/25.

https://turmericlife.com/blogs/news/turmeric-recipes-golden-paste?s. Accessed 9/2/25.

https://turmericlife.com/pages/about-dr-doug-turmeric-life. Accessed 9/2/25.

https://turmericlife.com/blogs/news/turmeric-citrus-wellness-shot-recipe-by-dr-doug. Accessed 9/2/25.

https://turmericlife.com.au/blogs/news/dont-drink-turmeric-heres-why. Accessed 9/2/25.

https://www.lisalise.com/shopblog/2021/10/11/how-to-make-a-self-preserving-turmeric-glycerite. Accessed 9/6/25.

https://willamettetransplant.com/turmeric-recipes/#recipes. Accessed 9/6/25.

https://www.verywellhealth.com/turmeric-shots-8784927. Accessed 9/8/25.

MacAller, Natasha. *Spice Health Heroes*. Jacqui Small, 2016.

Madison, Deborah. *Vegetarian Cooking for Everyone*. Broadway Books, 1997.

Ginger and turmeric are often used together in many Asian dishes.
Susan Belsinger

Cooking with Turmeric

Pat Crocker

I love cooking with turmeric and use it almost every day. Do I love it because it's a powerful healer? Most definitely, yes! I also love the gingery-citrus aroma, the golden hue it imparts to everything, and of course, its complex, warm, slightly musky, and earthy taste that harmonizes so well with many other herbs and spices.

The fleshy, bright orange rhizomes, which can be grated into curry blends and pastes, sauces and dips, are the very best form to use in cooking. Fresh, raw turmeric contains a higher concentration of curcumin compared to dried or powdered forms, which is why I often juice the fresh root along with oranges, melon, and all kinds of other fruit.

Look for fresh turmeric at large, well-stocked grocery stores, some whole/health food or Asian grocery stores. Choose firm rhizomes with light brown skin and bright orange flesh. Always peel fresh turmeric and ginger before using in recipes. Although harder to find, turmeric roots are also preserved in syrup and ground into paste, sometimes with other herbs and/or honey. I've included recipes for both sweet and savory Turmeric Paste.

Both fresh and dried turmeric lend a bright yellow color to rice, scrambled eggs, potato dishes, or frittata. If you grow turmeric, you will be rewarded with fresh leaves that can be added to soup stock or sauce like you would bay leaves, and tender fresh shoots that can be eaten like asparagus. Turmeric leaves can be soaked and used to wrap fish, vegetables, or rice for steaming, because they lend a subtle, citrusy-tart flavor.

Convenient to buy and easy to use, dried, powdered, grated, or less common, crushed, turmeric is warm and musky but slightly more bitter in taste than fresh. Dried, grated or powdered turmeric is used in sauces, pickle seasoning, relish and mustard, or with vegetable or meat curries. Add powdered turmeric to juice or smoothies and to prepared mayonnaise, relishes or other condiments to boost their healthful quality.

Turmeric complements beans, eggplant, eggs, fish, lentils, poultry, beef, rice, potatoes and other root vegetables, and greens such as cabbage and spinach. In spice blends, soups, sauces, or vegetable dishes, turmeric combines well with chile, cilantro, cloves, coconut milk, coriander, cumin, fennel, garlic, ginger, lime and lemon juice and zest, mustard seeds, pepper and parsley.

Savory Red Turmeric Paste

This version is hot, but you can adjust the heat by reducing or removing the cayenne peppers. Keep the black pepper, which is always included with turmeric because it may help the body to absorb its inflammation-busting compounds.

Fenugreek lends a curry flavor to spice blends. You can use more fenugreek for a stronger curry taste.

Savory Red Turmeric Paste. *Pat Crocker*

I love having this spice paste on hand because it makes my cooking life easy—easy to flavor-spike scrambled eggs, soups, roasting vegetables, and even salad dressings. Try whisking a tablespoon (or less if you're spice-shy) into onions as they are sautéing or into liquids for any dish that needs oomph.

Makes about 1 cup

10 fresh red cayenne peppers, stemmed and seeded
3 cloves garlic, minced
1 piece (2-inch) fresh turmeric, grated
1 piece (1-inch) fresh ginger, grated
1/4 cup roasted red pepper, chopped
6 sprigs fresh cilantro or flat-leaf parsley
1 tablespoon lemon or lime zest
1 teaspoon Malabar black peppercorns, cracked
1 teaspoon coriander seeds, ground
1 teaspoon fenugreek seeds, ground, optional
1/2 teaspoon sea salt

In a food processor, combine cayenne peppers, garlic, turmeric and ginger and pulse until finely chopped. Add roasted red pepper, cilantro or parsley, and zest. Process until peppers are finely chopped. Add peppercorns, coriander, fenugreek, if using, and salt. Process for 20 seconds.

With the motor running, add the sesame oil, one tablespoon at a time, through the opening in the lid. Process and add more oil until a smooth paste is achieved. Use less oil for a dry paste and more oil for a softer paste.

Transfer to a small jar with tight-fitting lid and label. Store in a sealed container in the refrigerator for up to 2 months.

Sweet Turmeric Paste

Pop a couple teaspoons of this paste (or the Savory Red Paste) into the water before cooking rice or pasta for a fragrantly spiced product. The taste is smooth, and it subtly warms both sweet and savory dishes.

Makes about 1/2 cup

1 piece (2-inches) fresh turmeric, grated
1 piece (1-inch) fresh ginger, grated
1 teaspoon cumin seeds
1 teaspoon coriander seeds
1 tablespoon crushed cinnamon stick or 2 tablespoons ground cinnamon
2 teaspoons fenugreek seeds, optional
2 to 3 tablespoons honey or maple syrup
1/2 teaspoon sea salt

In a blender or small food processor, combine turmeric, ginger, cumin, coriander, cinnamon, and fenugreek, if using. Process until mixture is smooth and fairly fine.

Drizzle honey or maple syrup over, 1 tablespoon at a time, and process in food processor until a smooth paste is achieved. Add salt and pulse to mix well.

Transfer to a small jar with tight-fitting lid and label. Store in a sealed container, at room temperature up to 2 weeks or in the refrigerator for up to 3 months.

Sweet Turmeric Paste. *Susan Belsinger*

Gingerbread Spice Blend

If I could only have one spice blend, this would be it because it's so versatile, not just for using in gingerbread, pudding, cake, or cookie recipes. Use it in drinks such as eggnog, latté, or fruit smoothies; and when combined with granulated sugar, it's a tasty rim duster. It also complements savory or sweet squash or pumpkin recipes, and it flavors the Crumble recipe, below. Keep it handy to sprinkle over puddings or applesauce or into soups, dressings, or sauces.

Makes about 1/3 cup

2 tablespoons ground cinnamon
2 tablespoons ground ginger
1 tablespoon ground turmeric
1 teaspoon ground allspice
1 teaspoon ground nutmeg
1 teaspoon ground black pepper
1/2 teaspoon sea salt
1/4 teaspoon ground cloves

Combine all ingredients in a small bowl and mix well. Transfer to a small jar with tight-fitting lid and label. Store at room temperature for 5 to 6 months.

Turmeric or Ginger Honey

You can use turmeric or ginger in this delicious honey. I prefer the turmeric version and if you're worried that it might be somewhat overpowering, or that it will change the taste of the honey, fear not. The turmeric actually complements the honey and it is so versatile. I've drizzled it over yogurt, ice cream, and pound cake, and spooned it into tea.

It's divine with Chai Tea—and in smoothies. Add a drop to sauces and dressings where just a spark of sweetness brightens the taste. It's used in the Turmeric Pineapple Pancakes, below. If you keep it on the counter, you will find many different ways to use this delicious sweetener.

It's important to thoroughly beat the oil into the honey; once it is completely mixed in, it won't separate. To bring the honey back to a pourable liquid, sit the jar in a small saucepan of boiling water that reaches 2/3 of the way up the jar. After a couple of minutes, using potholders, lift the jar out of the water.

Makes 3/4 cup

1/2 cup raw liquid honey
3 tablespoons coconut oil, warmed to liquid
1 tablespoon dried, ground turmeric or ginger
1/4 teaspoon ground black pepper

Combine honey, oil, turmeric or ginger, and pepper in a bowl. Using a long-handled spoon or whisk, beat the mixture until the oil is completely blended into the honey.

Transfer to a glass jar with a tight-fitting lid and label. Store in a sealed container at room temperature.

Turmeric complements the flavor of honey in this versatile sweetener.
Pat Crocker

Turmeric Pineapple Pancakes

More than just pancakes, these are a special, weekend kind of treat. Use the reserved juice to make breakfast smoothies or to add to soup stock as it simmers on the stove.

Swap 1 teaspoon ground turmeric and 2 teaspoons ground cinnamon for the Sweet Turmeric Paste. You could also try 1 tablespoon Savory Red Turmeric Paste for more zing.

Makes 4 to 6 servings

1 small, fresh pineapple or canned pineapple slices
1/2 cup unbleached flour
1 1/2 teaspoons baking powder
Pinch sea salt
3/4 cup almond milk
2 tablespoons Sweet Turmeric Paste or 1 teaspoon ground turmeric and 2 teaspoons ground cinnamon
1 large egg, beaten
1 tablespoon coconut oil, melted
1/4 cup Turmeric Honey, recipe above or regular honey or maple syrup
Butter or oil for greasing the skillet

Preheat oven to 300°F and lightly oil a baking sheet.

Cut and discard top and outer rind away from pineapple. Slice into 1/2-inch thick slices. Drain and save juice (for another use) from canned slices if using. Pat slices dry with a clean tea (or paper) towel.

Sift flour, baking powder, and salt into a large mixing bowl.

Whisk together milk, Sweet Turmeric Paste, egg, and oil in a small bowl. Make a well in the center of the dry ingredients and pour in the wet ingredients. Beat with a fork just enough to make a smooth batter.

Lightly oil a large skillet and heat over medium heat. Spoon a couple of tablespoons of batter into the skillet and spread around, adding more if necessary so that each pancake is slightly larger than the pineapple slices. Repeat so that you have 2 to 3 well-spaced pancakes in the skillet.

Lightly push one pineapple slice onto each pancake in the skillet and cook until bubbles appear in the pancakes and the edges are set. Carefully flip each pancake over and cook for a couple of minutes or until pineapple is lightly browned. Remove to the baking sheet, cover with foil, and keep warm in preheated oven.

Repeat process until all the pineapple slices have been used. Serve hot and pass honey to drizzle over top.

Best consumed immediately or tightly wrapped and refrigerated for 1 day.

Turmeric-Chickpea Crumble

Consider this to be a gluten-free alternative to breadcrumbs and you will begin to see all sorts of possibilities for using it. Chop the mixture fine and use it in place of breadcrumbs when making meatloaf or meatballs (or their vegetable counterpart), or as a coating for breading chicken, schnitzels, potatoes or zucchini for air frying. Coarsely chop it for use as a bread-free base for stuffing chicken, tomatoes, or peppers. You can also use it as a crunchy salad topping or for all kinds of casseroles, soups, and stews.

Makes about 1 1/4 cups

1 can (19-oz) or 2 cups cooked chickpeas, rinsed and drained
1/2 cup raw pistachio nuts, pumpkin seeds or almonds
2 tablespoons extra-virgin olive oil
1 tablespoon Gingerbread Spice Blend, above, or 1 teaspoon each: ground turmeric, cinnamon, and ginger
1/2 teaspoon sea salt

Line a rimmed baking sheet with parchment paper and preheat oven to 350°F.

Pat chickpeas dry and combine with nuts in a food processor. Pulse for 30 seconds or until coarsely chopped. Scrape into a medium bowl and add oil, spice blend or turmeric, cinnamon, ginger, and salt. Toss well to coat with oil and herbs.

Spread in one layer on prepared baking sheet. Bake in preheated oven for 30 minutes or until crunchy. Remove, set aside on a cooling rack to cool completely before storing.

Store in a sealed container for up to 15 days in a cool cupboard or for up to 2 months in the freezer.

Curried Vegetables

This dish is relatively mildly spicy; so, if you really like heat and spice, taste and add more Red Turmeric Paste. There is fresh turmeric in the paste, but you can add more if desired.

It's a great recipe for using up vegetables you already have in the refrigerator because you can swap a parsnip for the carrot and Brussels sprouts or green beans for the broccoli. Chopped cabbage works just as well in place of the cauliflower.

Cherry tomatoes add pops of color and flavor, but you can also use 2 tomatoes, skinned and chopped, or 1/4 cup tomato sauce instead.

Serves 4

2 tablespoons plus one tablespoon extra-virgin olive oil
1 onion, chopped
1 leek, sliced
1 cup cherry tomatoes, halved
2 cloves garlic, minced
1 tablespoon Savory Red Turmeric Paste, or purchased ground curry blend
1 inch fresh turmeric, finely chopped, optional
1 can (15 ounce) coconut milk
1 carrot, cut crosswise into coins
1 cup broccoli florets
1/2 head cauliflower, cut into 1-inch slices
Salt to taste

Heat 2 tablespoons oil in a large skillet over medium-high heat. Add onion and leek. Cook, stirring frequently for 5 minutes or until soft and translucent. Add remaining tablespoon oil and stir in tomatoes, garlic, Red Turmeric Paste, and turmeric, if using.

Cook, stirring frequently for 3 minutes.

Add coconut milk and bring to a light boil. Stir in carrot, broccoli, and cauliflower. Reduce heat, cover, and simmer for 12 minutes or until vegetables are crisp-tender. Taste and add salt if required.

Make it a Bowl: For each serving, spoon one cup Curried Vegetables over 1/2 cup cooked brown rice. Garnish with Turmeric-Chickpea Crumble, above if desired.

Store in a sealed container, in the refrigerator for up to 3 days; in the freezer for up to 2 months.

Curried Vegetables. *Pat Crocker*

Chicken and Bean Hash

This is a great weeknight meal. It doesn't really need the eggs, so often I serve it over cooked grains (rice or pasta or quinoa) without the eggs. It is also great over mashed or baked potatoes. Serve with a salad or green vegetable or add chopped broccoli or cauliflower with the onions. It's a tasty, easy dinner to improvise and make your own.

For a vegetarian option, substitute 2 cups chopped tofu or mushrooms in place of chicken.

Makes 4 to 6 servings

2 tablespoons + 4 teaspoons cold-pressed olive oil, divided
1 onion, thinly sliced
2 cloves garlic, finely chopped
1 tablespoon fresh ginger, finely chopped
1 tablespoon fresh turmeric, finely chopped
1 teaspoon smoked paprika
1/2 teaspoon Harissa, or hot sauce, optional
1 pound ground chicken
1 can (540 mL) cannellini or white kidney beans, drained
4 eggs, optional
1/4 cup Turmeric Chickpea Crumble, optional, for garnish

Chicken and Bean Hash. *Pat Crocker*

Heat 2 tablespoons oil in a large skillet over medium-high heat. Add onion and cook, stirring frequently for 5 minutes or until soft and transparent. Stir in garlic, ginger, turmeric, paprika, and Harissa or hot sauce, if using; and cook, stirring constantly for 2 minutes.

Add chicken to the pan, breaking it up with the back of a wooden spoon. Cook, stirring frequently for 5 minutes or until all traces of pink have disappeared. Stir beans into the pan and mix in well.

If using eggs, make 4 wells in the mixture and drop 1 teaspoon of oil into each. Break an egg into each well and cook, flipping once; cover until eggs are set.

For each serving, spoon one cup of the bean mixture onto a plate. Lift one egg from the pan onto the bean mixture and garnish with a tablespoon of the Chickpea Crumble, if using.

Serve immediately; if necessary, store in a sealed container and use within 1 or 2 days.

Spiced Chocolate Mousse

I love that this sweet treat has healthy amino fatty acids (from the avocado), it's sooooooo easy to make, and it is also gluten-free and vegan. What else could you ask for?

I use the full-strength Savory Red Turmeric Paste, but you can go with Sweet Turmeric Paste or the Gingerbread Spice Blend. This recipe makes 2 servings, so if you're feeding 4 people, you can double it, and try two different spice blends and compare tastes.

Makes 2 servings

1 large ripe avocado
1/4 cup natural dark cocoa powder
3 tablespoons almond milk
2 tablespoons maple syrup
1 tablespoon Savory Red Turmeric Paste or Sweet Turmeric Paste
Kosher salt and shaved chocolate for garnishing

Combine milk, syrup, avocado, cocoa, and Turmeric Paste in a blender or food processor. Process on high for 30 seconds or until mixture is smooth.

Scrape into 2 small bowls, garnish with salt and chocolate and refrigerate for 30 minutes or until chilled.

Serve as soon as chilled. If necessary, store in a sealed container and use within 1 or 2 days.

Pat Crocker's mission in life is to write with insight and experience, cook with playful abandon, and eat herbs with gusto. She is happiest in a kitchen or sharing what she knows about herbs, whole foods, and eating to be healthy. In fact, Pat infuses the medicinal benefits of herbs in every original recipe she develops.

A professional Home Economist (BAA, Toronto Metropolitan University) and Culinary Herbalist, Pat's passion for healthy food is fueled by her knowledge and love of herbs—she grows, photographs, and writes about what she calls *the helping plants*.

An award-winning author—she received the Herb Society of America Award for Excellence in Herbal Literature—Pat has written 23 herb/healthy cookbooks, including *The Herbalist's Kitchen*, *The Healing Herbs Cookbook*, and *The Juicing Bible*.
www.patcrocker.com

Northern Thailand Curried Noodles. *Rosemary Davis*

Savory Turmeric Recipes

Rosemary Davis

Northern Thailand Curried Noodles (*khao soi*)

This dish is embedded in the cuisine of Northern Thailand. There is debate as to whether it originated in the Shan State of Myanmar (Burma) or came into Thailand with Muslim spice traders from the Yunnan Province of China. Regardless of origin, it is a rich and delicious one-dish meal.

The choice of protein here is up to the cook. Traditionally it is made with beef, but chicken, shrimp, or tofu could be substituted as well, with slightly reduced cooking time compared to beef.

Yields 4 servings

4 cloves peeled, minced garlic
1-inch piece fresh turmeric, peeled and minced, or 1 tablespoon ground turmeric
1 tablespoon red curry paste
3 cups canned unsweetened coconut milk
3/4-pound boneless tender beef, such as sirloin tips, cubed
1 tablespoon sugar
3 tablespoons Thai fish sauce
3 tablespoons lime juice
1 pound Chinese egg noodles (other pasta types may be substituted)
Salt to taste
1 to 2 tablespoons peanut oil or olive oil for sautéing
Suggested garnishes:
Crispy fried shallots, minced scallions, minced cilantro, or finely shredded cabbage

In a small bowl, blend the minced garlic, minced or powdered turmeric, and curry paste.

In a heavy skillet or saucepan over medium-high heat, heat 1 to 2 tablespoons of oil and sauté the garlic-turmeric-curry paste mixture for 30 seconds. Add half the coconut milk, reduce heat to medium, and simmer for 5 minutes.

Add the meat and sugar and cook for 5 to 7 minutes. Add the remaining coconut milk, fish sauce, and salt; simmer for 10 minutes. Remove from the heat, add the lime juice, and set aside.

Boil the noodles in a large pot of salted water according to package directions and drain. Divide the noodles into serving bowls and spoon the curry mixture over. Garnish as desired. Chopsticks and large spoons are recommended to slurp up all the turmeric-laced goodness.

Persian Grilled Fish with Dates *(Sabour mashwi)*

This dish from the Persian Gulf is best grilled over an open flame but can also be baked in the oven. A whole fish such as a red snapper would be perfect here, but other whole fish or fish filets of your choice—preferably skin-on—may be substituted. The spice mix can be made ahead as a pantry staple.

Yield: 6 servings

Kuwaiti Spice Mix

This regional spice mix is best when you grind the spices yourself.

1/2 cup mixed peppercorns
1/4 cup cayenne pepper
1 1/2 teaspoons each: coriander, cumin, ginger, cinnamon, cloves, and nutmeg

Grind the spices yourself in a coffee grinder, or mix pre-ground spices. Store the blend in an airtight jar for up to six months.

Persian Fish

One five-to-six-pound whole fish, cleaned and scaled, head and tail on, or equal amount of fish fillets
1 1/2 pounds of dates, soaked in water for two hours, soaking liquid reserved
1 tablespoon Kuwaiti Spice Mix

2 cups chopped cilantro
1/2 pound chopped onions
12 cloves minced garlic
1/4 cup chopped fresh dill
2 tablespoons ground turmeric
Grated zest and juice of 2 limes
Salt and pepper to taste
2 tablespoons olive oil
Chopped parsley for garnish

Place the dates and their soaking liquid in a food processor or blender and process to a paste. Add a little more water if necessary.

If using a whole fish, rub the Kuwaiti Spice Mixture all over the inside and outside of the fish. If using fillets, rub on all sides.

Mix the cilantro, onions, garlic, dill, turmeric, lime, salt, pepper, olive oil and date paste in a bowl. If using a whole fish, pack the cavity and spread the outside with the paste, then tie the fish shut with kitchen twine if it will be grilled. If using filets, rub the mixture on all sides.

For best flavor, put the dressed fish (whole or filets) in the refrigerator for 3 to 4 hours. Grill or bake in a preheated 400° oven until the fish starts to flake when pricked with a fork, about 45 minutes.

Cambodian Yellow Spice Paste (*Kroeung*)

This vibrant flavoring paste is essential to Khmer cuisine and, like all Thai curry pastes, can be varied to the individual cook's taste. A "green" paste might be heavier on herbs; a "red" paste might include hot chiles. This one is a "yellow" kroeung, due to the turmeric.

It is excellent used as a marinade for anything that will fit on a skewer, or used as a condiment with stir-fried dishes, noodles, and soups.

Note: Frozen minced lemongrass is available in most Asian groceries if you cannot find fresh.

Yields 3/4 cup

2 stalks fresh lemongrass or 3 tablespoons thawed minced lemongrass
8 cloves garlic, peeled and chopped
1 to 2 shallots, chopped
1 ounce fresh turmeric root, peeled and chopped, or two heaping tablespoons ground turmeric
1 ounce fresh ginger root, peeled and chopped, or two heaping tablespoons ground ginger
3 tablespoons fresh lime juice
1 teaspoon kosher salt or sea salt
2 to 3 tablespoons of sesame, peanut or olive oil

If using fresh lemongrass, trim the tough root ends of the stalks and trim the tops; remove the toughest outer leaves. Roughly chop the stalks.

Blend all the paste ingredients in a food processor or blender.

Store in an airtight jar in the refrigerator for 5 to 7 days, with a little extra oil drizzled on top to prevent oxidation. The paste may also be frozen.

Chai Spice Mix. *Karen England*

Drink Up! Homemade Turmeric Chai Concentrate

Karen England

Thirty years ago, I was introduced to the International Herb Association and the Herb of the Year program by my friend Theresa Loe. She and I have been IHA members on and off since that time, with me being the one "on" currently. Then, twenty years ago, Theresa introduced me to a drink called *Chai,* something I had never heard of before. She taught me to make a Chai Concentrate that I have expanded upon over the years and share with you now, with her full permission and blessing.

Chai Spice Mix

The following ingredients will make one batch of dry mix that will make either 4 cups of the liquid Chai Concentrate or 1 cup of Chai-Infused Vodka.

Makes about 1/2 cup

1/3 cup coconut sugar or dark brown sugar
2 tablespoons loose black tea leaves such as Darjeeling
2 teaspoons ground turmeric
1 teaspoon dried red rose petals
1/2 teaspoon each ground ginger, cardamom, and cinnamon
1/4 teaspoon ground allspice
6 whole cloves
6 whole black peppercorns
3 dried bay leaves, crumbled
1/4 vanilla bean, cut in half lengthwise

Start by making the dry mix—toss all ingredients in a bowl and mix well.

Chai Concentrate

To make the liquid chai concentrate, combine the above mix in a small saucepan with 4 cups of filtered water, barely bring to a boil; reduce heat to a simmer for 10 minutes. Turn off the heat, cover the saucepan, and cool completely. Strain into a glass jar or container for storage. Label and keep refrigerated.

To use the concentrate to make individual chai drinks that can be served hot or cold:

Combine equal parts liquid chai concentrate and filtered water for a cup of tea. If desired, add sweetener of choice to taste and serve with a splash of milk or cream.

Combine equal parts liquid chai concentrate and milk of choice such as coconut or almond milk for a chai latte or chai golden milk. Speaking of golden milk, I have it on good authority that the president of the IHA likes to drink her golden milk hot, with dark chocolate chips melted in the bottom of her mug! So, guess how I like mine?

Chai Golden Milk. *Karen England*

Chai-Infused Vodka

To make chai-infused vodka for cocktails, in a pint-size mason jar combine 1/2 cup of the dry mix with one cup of 80- or 100-proof vodka, seal tightly with a lid and shake to fully combine. Set aside at room temperature for several days and shake occasionally before using in cocktails.

I don't strain this right away, because I like it to continue to get stronger and stronger; so I strain it as I use it. Feel free to strain it, discarding the spicy bits, as soon as it is strong enough to your taste.

Have you ever heard of a cocktail called a White Russian? It's an easy, classic, three-ingredient drink consisting of vodka, Kahlúa and cream, in which the cream makes it white and the vodka makes it Russian supposedly. One popular variation of the drink is a Chai White Russian, essentially taking out the coffee-flavored Kahlúa and substituting instead Chai flavoring. I think many of the recipes for chai versions of a White Russian cocktail can be a bit flat, especially with only a few ingredients—so here's my take on the drink that I like to call the Golden Russian, utilizing more ingredients including the Chai Concentrate and Chai-Infused Vodka to obtain an unbelievably delicious cocktail year-round—refreshing when served cold in warm weather, and comforting when served hot in cold weather.

Golden Russian

Makes 4 x 3-ounce drinks

Note: 1 ounce equals 2 tablespoons

2 ounces plain vodka
2 ounces Chai-Infused Vodka, strained
2 ounces gin, such as London dry (if you don't like gin, you could use 2 more ounces of plain vodka, but the gin really plays well with the spices in this version so give it a try!)
2 ounces liquid Chai Concentrate
1/2 to 1 ounce (1 to 2 tablespoons) homemade vanilla extract, or store-bought pure vanilla extract, to taste (*Homemade vanilla extract may be not as strong as store-bought, so the larger amount applies to homemade.*)
1/2 to 1 ounce maple syrup, depending on how sweet you want the drink
2 ounces heavy cream, or canned coconut cream or coconut milk

For the cold version, in an 18-ounce or larger jug or jar, combine the vodkas, gin if using, chai concentrate, vanilla extract, maple syrup, and cream. Stir to mix the cocktail ingredients well in the jug.

Fill 4 Old-Fashioned cocktail glasses with fresh ice made with filtered water and pour equal amounts of the cocktail from the jug into each glass.

Garnish with a sprinkling of ground turmeric and freshly grated black pepper and/or dried red rose petals, optional.

For a hot version, warm all the ingredients in a saucepan (or a crockpot) until steaming and serve in warmed mugs.

Karen England lives, works, and gardens on two steeply sloping acres in Vista, a small town in northern San Diego County, California, just nine miles as a crow flies from the Pacific Ocean. When she's not drinking herbal cocktails, she drinks tea.

Find her on Instagram @edgehillherbfarm.

Golden Russian. *Karen England*

Turmeric Recipes for Every Day

Carol Little

Turmeric is an herb we need to know and use. Yes, it's the rich yellowy mustard colour in curry powder and it is gaining popularity as one of the heavy hitters of herbal medicine. I hope that these ideas will inspire you and enable you to embrace this very special herbal ally—to enjoy in your "everyday." Note: Always use organic turmeric whenever possible.

Homemade Golden Milk Powder

Makes about 1/4 cup herb powder

3 tablespoons ground turmeric
2 teaspoons ground Ceylon cinnamon
1 teaspoon fennel
1/2 teaspoon cloves
1/4 teaspoon organic ground cardamom
1/2 teaspoon organic ground black pepper, optional
1 teaspoon gingerroot powder, optional

Combine the herbs and spices. Store in an airtight container and label.

Add a teaspoon or tablespoon (depending on your preference) to a mug of warmed milk, or milk with a shot of Expresso coffee. Use a milk frother if available to make it even more delightful!

Aromatic Turmeric Chai Latte

I like to pour coconut milk into a small bowl and mix well as often the milk/cream can separate in the can. It's best to heat the mixture slowly so that the coconut milk doesn't thicken up too much. Any of these are delicious. Experiment or pick your own options. (Your choice/taste as to the amount of turmeric—start lower and increase amount as you go.)

Yields about 1 cup

1 cup coconut milk or oat, almond or your favorite milk
1/2 teaspoon to 2 teaspoons turmeric powder
1/2 teaspoon cinnamon powder
1/8 teaspoon nutmeg, grated fresh
1/8 teaspoon fresh black pepper or about 3 'grinds'

Optional add-ons:
Dash of cayenne pepper
Raw honey or maple syrup to taste
1/2 teaspoon of coconut oil or ghee
2 star anise
2 to 3 cardamom pods

Combine all ingredients (except honey if using) in a medium-size pot and warm slowly, stirring often. Allow to come to a simmer. Pour into a mug and top with a little more grated nutmeg or a sprinkle of cinnamon if you like. Froth it up a little with a fork or if you have a little frothy gizmo.

Tropical Smoothie with Turmeric

Throw it all together in a blender and blend away!

Yields about 2 cups

1 cup coconut milk
1/2 cup frozen mango chunks (or pineapple)
1 tablespoon coconut oil
1 frozen banana
1 teaspoon chia seeds
2 grinds black pepper

1/2 teaspoon cinnamon powder
1/2 teaspoon ginger (grated, fresh if possible)
1 teaspoon fresh grated turmeric or 1/2 teaspoon turmeric powder

Sunshine in a Glass

Serves 3 to 4

Fresh turmeric, about 1-inch in length, peeled or 1 teaspoon powdered turmeric
Fresh ginger root, 1- to 2-inch piece, peeled if not organic, or 1 teaspoon powdered ginger
1 frozen banana, chopped
1 cup fresh mango, cut into chunks
2 to 3 grinds fresh pepper
1 cup coconut milk or almond milk or any milk
1 teaspoon vanilla extract, optional

Variations--add the following:
1 teaspoon chia seeds
1/2 teaspoon cinnamon powder

Toss all ingredients in a blender or VitaMix and whiz up.

Turmeric Dip

I love this dip so much—I hope you do too! To use toasted over raw seeds— lightly toast the sesame seeds ahead of time and allow them to cool before adding—I have used and like both. Serve with raw or baked veggies, or the dip can become a scrumptious salad dressing.

Yields approximately 2/3 cup

1/2 cup organic tahini
1/4 cup lemon juice
1 tablespoon raw honey
2 1/2 teaspoons turmeric powder
2 cloves garlic, minced
Dash sea salt
1/4 teaspoon ground black pepper

Sesame seeds to garnish (raw or lightly toasted)
Fresh cilantro, finely chopped, optional garnish

In a blender, combine the tahini, lemon juice, honey, turmeric and garlic. Blend until smooth. Taste and season with salt and pepper. Check for desired thickness; you may want to add up to 1/4 cup warm water (or a bit little less, to obtain the thickness desired).

Transfer to a bowl and top with a light dusting of sesame seeds. Add the cilantro, if using.

No-Bake Snacks with Turmeric

This is more of a template than a recipe. So many wonderful options. Just choose the ingredients you prefer and follow the amounts. We can make these kinds of 'balls' for so many reasons. I make many variations of this recipe dependent upon the intent of this tasty medicine.

This can be such a fun project with any 'small fry' in your home.

Makes about 12 balls

1/2 cup organic toasted, unsalted cashews (or your favourite nut)
1/2 cup organic, unsweetened dried apricots (or your favourite dried fruit)
3 teaspoons homemade Golden Milk Powder
1/4 cup organic coconut flakes (plus extra for coating, if desired)
1/2 cup pitted Medjool dates (about 6 dates)
1/4 cup organic cashew butter (or your favourite nut butter)
2 tablespoons maple syrup
1 teaspoon organic fractionated (MCT) coconut oil, optional

Add the cashews into the food processor and pulse until finely ground. Add the apricots and pulse to combine. Add the Golden Milk Powder and the coconut flakes. Blend well to mix. Add them into fruit and nut mixture, pulse to combine well.

Turn the food processor on low and gradually add cashew butter and maple syrup (as well as the MCT if using).

Break apart small chunks of the dough with your hands and make 1-inch balls. Set aside on a plate or baking sheet covered with parchment paper.

Roll the balls gently and place on the baking sheet.

Place in the fridge immediately for 2 to 3 hours to set up. Store in fridge for up to 2 weeks, or freeze and use within 3 months. I tend to use a cookie tin and separate the layers with parchment paper.

Autumn Veggie Bake with Turmeric

Yields about 6 cups (1.5 litres); 3 to 4 servings as a main dish, or 4 to 6 servings as a side.

1 medium-size onion, diced
2 tablespoons olive oil
1 tablespoon turmeric powder
1 tablespoon curry powder
Sea salt
Freshly ground black pepper.
Sprinkle hot chile flakes, optional
3 sweet potatoes, diced
3 cups cauliflower, chopped bite-sized
1 can chickpeas, drained and rinsed
1/2 cup vegetable or chicken stock
2 spicy sausages, finely chopped, optional

In a skillet, sauté onions in the olive oil, until softened. Sprinkle turmeric, curry, salt, pepper and hot chile flakes (if using) into the onions. Stir well until blended.

Add the sweet potatoes, cauliflower and chickpeas. Mix well. Add the vegetable or chicken stock; mix. Add the sausage, if using, and combine thoroughly.

Preheat oven to 350°F. Prepare a couple of baking sheets. Either grease lightly with butter or oil, or use parchment paper or foil to cover them. Gently pour the mixture onto the baking sheets, ensuring everything is spread out evenly if possible. Bake in hot oven for 30 to 35 minutes.

Serve your golden soup with bread or croutons. *Susan Belsinger*

Golden Goddess Sunshine Soup

Adapted in honour of my dear departed friend and fab chef Fernand. For a vegan version—leave out the cream and add 1 tablespoon 'Bragg's Liquid Aminos' if desired.

If you want to thin out this very luscious soup, I suggest adding some veggie or bone broth. Serve with a swirl of lime zest and your choice of crusty bread or gluten free crackers.

Yields about 8 cups (2 litres) of soup (4 to 6 servings)

3 sweet potatoes, peeled and chopped
3 to 4 carrots, peeled and chopped (if organic, don't peel)
1 butternut squash, peeled and cubed
4 cups orange juice
1 to 2 tablespoons fresh gingerroot, grated
1 tablespoon turmeric powder or 2 tablespoons fresh grated turmeric root
1 teaspoon freshly grated nutmeg

1/8 teaspoon sea salt
1/4 teaspoon fresh ground pepper
1 tablespoon citrus rind zest (orange, lemon, lime, or combination)
1 teaspoon lime peel zest for garnish
1 cup 5% cream; substitute coconut milk or your favourite alternative dairy, optional

Prepare the vegetables. Put the orange juice in a large stainless pot and add the vegetables. Bring to a boil. Turn down the heat and allow to simmer until soft, about 20 minutes. Add the seasonings and blend until smooth with an immersion blender; add cream and taste for seasoning. Serve with lime zest garnish.

Savoury Chicken Skillet

Serve with your favourite rice, quinoa or grain or my latest thing—serve slathered over warm, prepared spaghetti squash.

Yields about 4 cups (1 litre); 3 to 4 servings

2 tablespoons unsalted butter
1 medium onion, very thinly sliced
1 tablespoon fresh turmeric root, peeled and minced
1/4 teaspoon freshly ground black pepper
1/2 teaspoon sea salt, plus more for seasoning
1 1/2 pounds boneless, skinless chicken thighs
1 1/2 teaspoons ground turmeric
1/2 cup dry white wine
1/2 cup chicken broth
1/2 cup coconut cream (or your choice of milk)
Chopped cilantro, basil or flat leaf parsley for garnish

Melt the butter in a large pan over medium heat. Add the onion, fresh turmeric, pepper, and 1/2 teaspoon of the salt. Cook, stirring occasionally, until the onions are softened, about 5 minutes.

Place the chicken on a plate, sprinkle it with salt and the ground turmeric and set aside.

Move the onions to the outer edges of the pan and place the chicken, seasoned-side down, in a single layer in the middle of the pan. Season the chicken with more salt. Cook until the chicken begins to brown, about 3 to 4 minutes. Turn the chicken with tongs and cook for another 2 minutes.

Pour in the wine and scrape the browned bits from the bottom of the pan. Cook for 1 minute, pour in the broth and the coconut milk and stir to mix.

Reduce heat to medium-low, cover, and cook until the chicken is tender and cooked through, 18 to 22 minutes. Serve with chopped fresh herbs as garnish.

Roasted Sweet Potatoes with Turmeric

This is so easy and tasty too. Substitute Yukon golds, carrots, parsnips or other root veggies. Sometimes, I simply add the potatoes, oil and spices (minus the salt) to a large zip-close bag, seal, and mix it all up there.

Yields about 6 cups (1.5 litres) of cooked sweet potatoes; 4 to 6 servings as a side dish.

4 to 5 sweet potatoes, peeled and diced into 1-inch cubes
1 teaspoon turmeric powder
1/2 teaspoon garam masala powder
2 tablespoons olive oil
1/2 teaspoon black pepper, freshly ground
1 teaspoon sea salt
Hot pepper flakes, chili powder, ancho chile powder or paprika, optional

Preheat oven to 400°F.

Place the diced sweet potatoes in a bowl and use a fork to rough up the edges a bit

Add the turmeric and garam masala to the olive oil and pour it over the sweet potatoes; grind the black pepper over the mixture. Stir to combine well or use your hands to mix it up until evenly coated. Place the sweet potatoes on a baking sheet and bake for 20 to 30 minutes.

Try to make sure potatoes are in a single layer, not touching, to ensure crispness. You can leave them to bake for the entire time or mix them halfway through. Once crisp and cooked (when they can be easily pierced with a fork), remove from the oven and add the sea salt and optional hot pepper flakes, chili powder, ancho chile powder or paprika.

Carol Little, R.H., is a traditional herbalist in Toronto, Cananda, where she has had a private practice for over 20 years. She loves to write about how we can incorporate herbs into our daily lives. Her easy-to-digest weekly blog posts offer quick takeaway ideas to help readers to feel their best. https://studiobotanica.com

Carol is a current professional and past board member of the Ontario Herbalists Association. She combines her love of travel and passion for all things green and enjoys writing about both. Carol has written for *Vitality Magazine* for many years. She is a regular contributor to the IHA annual Herb of the Year book. She is a proud participant in the much-loved *FIRE CIDER 101 Zesty Recipes for Health-Boosting Remedies* by Rosemary Gladstar and friends.

Carol's current project is a fun-filled "deep dive" into one herb each month— it's called HerbGals and is a creative and interactive way to learn about the many gifts and practical ways that we can embrace the green world. Herb enthusiasts, herbalists, gardeners, and those with culinary interests share and learn from each other!

For more information:
https://studiobotanica.teachable.com/p/herbgals
https://www.facebook.com/studiobotanica
https://instagram.com/studiobotanica

Skye's whimsical turmeric sprite. *Skye Suter*

Indian-Influenced Foods from My Childhood

Skye Suter

Turmeric, known as an herb and a spice, is a tuberous rhizome related to ginger, which it somewhat resembles. It is famously called the "Golden Spice" for its vibrant yellow color used to dye fabrics and foods. It has been important as medicinal herb throughout history. While turmeric has had a long and important history in the East, recognition and popularity came later in the Western ethos, as a supplement and superfood with antioxidant and anti-inflammatory properties. Turmeric has also had a "golden" history in cuisine, especially in Asian and Asian-inspired foods.

Many spice influences from childhood have shaped my tastes into adulthood, and I have a great affinity for highly spiced foods, including turmeric. Having spent my childhood years in India, I was exposed to a great deal of the country's indigenous cuisine as well as multicultural fusions. With influences flowing both ways, it was only natural for British and Dutch food cultures to be heavily influenced by the Indian table. Periods of colonialism led to many culinary exchanges, adaptations and the creation of new dishes.

Here in America, we have also embraced Indian food in a big way. Asian groceries and Indian restaurants can be found everywhere and offer us easy access to all kinds of prepared Indian foods, whether we want to eat out or do a takeaway. Asian markets offer many food products and spices, if one is moved to do some Indian cooking at home.

Individual spices and spice blends are readily available at Asian markets; these are a part of creating any curry dish. *Masala* is from the Hindi language and is a general term used to describe ground spice blends or mixes. There are endless variations, with some having specifically designated names like curry powder or *garam masala*. Curry powder is a yellow masala blending cumin, coriander, and plenty of turmeric with other spices. Garam masala is brown in color, and includes warm, intense spices like cardamom,

Indian cuisine uses a colorful array of spices. *Susan Belsinger*

cinnamon, cloves and nutmeg. The words curry and masala are often used interchangeably to define a curry dish, so sometimes a chicken curry may be called chicken masala. I often buy individual spices to create my own garam masalas at home to keep on hand for my next Indian dish. Recipes may be found in abundance on the internet, from your favorite cookbook or from your favorite Indian cook.

Turmeric and all the spices mentioned in the following recipes can be purchased at Asian and spice markets. Turmeric can be purchased as a powder by itself or mixed into a curry powder blend. It can also be purchased as a fresh rhizome and grated or sliced into recipes. Other spices like cardamom, cinnamon or cloves can be purchased whole or in powder form, as individual spices or as part of a masala. *Asafoetida* is a powdered resin that is added to dishes to impart unique Indian flavors to curries and such. For cooking use, the resin is compounded with flour into a fine powder. The smell of asafoetida has been described as peculiar or odiferous, but once it is added into the dish it dissipates. It is worth using but make sure to wrap it well before storing.

Many Asian markets also offer small kitchen appliances and utensils that help in the preparation of Indian dishes. In the days before blenders, food processors and spice grinders, Indian cooks (mostly housewives and hired cooks) would have to labor for hours, processing the ingredients for curries and masalas by hand. Whole spices and fresh ingredients like chile peppers, garlic and coriander leaves were crushed and mashed together with water in a mortar and pestle to form curry bases before they were put over the flame. Thank goodness for modern inventions!

Chicken curries in general are practically national dishes in Britain. Chicken Tikka Masala is a yogurt-based curry, which is less spicy than true Indian curries, created for the milder British palate. Mulligatawny soup is an Anglo-Indian dish consisting of a spicy broth, often with chicken, rice, lentils or chickpeas and spices. *Kedgeree* (from the Indian "Chichi") is a simple rice and lentil medley transformed during the British colonial period to include smoked haddock, boiled eggs and cream as a breakfast or brunch option.

In the Netherlands, the Dutch enjoy *Biryani* (rice with meat or vegetables), delicious tandoori chicken, various paneer (fresh cheese with a tofu-like texture) dishes, and many authentic curries and foods influenced by the spice traditions of India, Indonesia and other countries where there was a colonial presence. India felt the presence of The Dutch East India Company from 1605 to 1825. The Dutch occupied mostly southern and coastal areas of

India, like the region of Kerala. In the grand scheme of things, their time in India was relatively brief, but during that time they both brought in and took away culinary traditions from all over the world, intermingling Indo-Dutch cuisine and ideas with other countries, especially Indonesia, where they were prominently stationed.

I spent my formative years in India, where I was exposed to Anglo-Indian cuisine and other multicultural cuisine, as well as a lot of authentic Indian food. My father worked for the United States government, and we were stationed there for eight years. This gave me ample time to fully appreciate and acquire a deep affection for Indian food. When my brother and I were children, my mother would sometimes treat us to a *Rijsttafel* meal (a Dutch invention) featuring a curry, surrounded by a selection of side dishes. Mom served us egg curry over plain basmati rice and loaded the table with other accompaniments, which were meant to be spooned over or next to the curry, at the eater's discretion. Although there were endless options, Mom typically gave us little dishes of roasted cashews, golden raisins, a mint and cucumber Raita, sautéed onions, and one or two choices of chutneys, like apple and mango. She also gave us unsweetened coconut and baked bananas, both of which are direct influences from southern India. While Mom is unsure where she first ran across the concept for her Rijsttafel feast, I can only speculate that she discovered it through a Dutch connection at some US embassy party or other.

Kofta is another curry meal that my mother sometimes made for us. It is a curry with beef crumbled into the sauce, forming a texture similar to a Bolognese sauce, or with meatballs. like Swedish meatballs in sauce. My mother used to make Kofta styled with crumbled beef, while my sister-in-law Kiran makes it with tiny meatballs. Kiran hails from India, and she is a fantastic cook. I always hope to get a taste of some Indian food whenever we go visiting. Kiran gave me her recipe for Kofta with meatballs which can be found in this article.

Coronation Chicken

I am very fond of formal tea parties, complete with tiered trays filled with sweet and savory goodies and delightful, exotic teas. One of my favorite items served at these teas is a curry chicken salad sandwich. I always wanted to make it at home so I could eat some whenever I had a hankering for it.

When researching some recipes I found out that this very British chicken salad is called "Coronation Chicken." It was originally created for Queen

Elizabeth II's coronation luncheon as a cold chicken salad in 1953 and became a popular item served at afternoon teas. After consulting several recipes, I came up with my own, which has a lot of spicy flair, just the way I like it!

Colorful and tasty garnishes are a must for a pretty presentation. Use herb leaves such as chives, parsley, cilantro, or nasturtiums. Nasturtium petals or whole flowers are nice garnishes, as well as tiny flowers from rosemary or scented geraniums, and petals from chive flowers—anything in season.

Skye's Curry Chicken Salad

6 to 10 servings

2 1/2 to 3 cups roasted chicken, cubed, from 2 large breasts or a whole chicken
1/2 slivered almonds
1/2 cup sweetened dried cranberries (can substitute yellow raisins or fresh grapes)

Sauce

2 1/2 tablespoons curry powder
2 to 3 teaspoons turmeric
1 to 2 teaspoons mustard power
1/4 teaspoon garlic powder
1/2 to 1 teaspoon mushroom powder
2 teaspoons coriander seeds, crushed in a mortar
Freshly ground black pepper
Small pinch (or 2) ground cayenne
1/2 to 1 teaspoon garam masala, optional
1/2 to 1+ cup mayonnaise
Cut green onions, chives or other fresh herbs for garnish.
Herb flowers and/or leaves for garnish
Sandwich bread or croissants

Remove chicken from the bones of roasted whole chicken or chicken breasts. I like using a whole chicken; it is a bit more work, but the variety of pieces gives more flavor. Cube the chicken into bite-sized pieces and place in a bowl.

Give the almonds and dried cranberries a rough chop on the cutting board and add to the chicken. Stir to evenly distribute ingredients.

Place the curry powder, turmeric, mustard powder, garlic powder, mushroom powder, crushed coriander seeds, ground black pepper, cayenne, and garam masala in a separate bowl.

Add mayonnaise to the spices and combine. Taste the sauce and adjust spices to your liking. I do not have salt in this blend, because some things may already be salty, like the chicken, or spice blends like curry powder. When the taste is to your satisfaction, scrape and pour it into the cut up chicken and blend well. Add salt here, if you think it needs it.

Serving suggestions: For tea sandwiches, fill sliced bread with chicken salad, cut off the crusts, and cut into quarters. Finish with an herb leaf on top of each quarter and arrange on a plate for a high tea sandwich. For a bigger, but more calorie indulgent sandwich, cut a croissant in half lengthwise and fill it with the curry chicken salad. These may be cut in half. Serve with pretty herb flowers on the side.

Rijsttafel

"Rijsttafel" (pronounced /ˈraɪsˌtɑːfəl/ ry-stah-feil in English) is the name for a bountiful culinary spread featuring tasty dishes and small bites served with rice. The name comes from the Dutch, meaning "rice table" and originated in Indonesia. Rijsttafel is wildly popular in the Netherlands and Indonesia and with expats in India. A similar, though thoroughly Indian, presentation of foods called a Thali, which means plate or tray, incorporates many small portions of different foods served on a large tray or platter.

While India is overwhelmingly vegetarian, fish, meat and eggs are also consumed. My mother would serve her version of Rijsttafel with an egg curry as the centerpiece. Egg curries come in many styles and regional variations. Anda Masala and Dhaba Style Egg Curries hail from the north, while Kerala Egg Roast and Goan Egg Drop curry can be found in the South. There are endless egg curries from all over India.

Mom's Rijsttafel Featuring an Egg Curry

Serves 4 (2 eggs each)

1 teaspoon ghee or vegetable oil
8 hard-boiled eggs, peeled
1/8 teaspoon garam masala
1/8 teaspoon chili powder

In a large skillet, heat the ghee (or vegetable oil) over a medium heat and add the hard-boiled eggs. Swirl and turn the eggs around in the pan until golden and blistered. Remove from the pan, drain, and season with the garam masala and chili powder. Set aside for later.

Curry

1 tablespoon ghee or vegetable oil
1 to 2 teaspoons mustard seeds
1 cinnamon stick
2 to 3 cardamom pods
1 green chile or jalapeño, sliced lengthwise
1-inch piece fresh ginger, peeled and grated
4 medium garlic cloves, minced
1 large red onion, chopped
1 1/2 cups tomatoes, blanched to remove skins and coarsely chopped
1 tablespoon ground coconut
1 teaspoon ground turmeric
1 teaspoon ground coriander
1/2 teaspoon ground cumin
1/2 teaspoon garam masala, optional
1/2 teaspoon salt
1 teaspoon ground black pepper
1 1/2 cups water

In the same pan, melt the tablespoon of ghee, over medium low, then add the mustard seeds. After they start popping, add the cinnamon stick, cardamom pods and green chile. After frying for a minute or so add the ginger and garlic, then the onions and tomatoes. Sauté for 8 to 10 minutes, until onion is wilted and translucent and tomatoes have broken down.

Remove the cinnamon stick and cardamom pods; discard.

Add the coconut, turmeric, coriander, cumin, garam masala, salt and pepper. Add the water and stir; cook for 5 minutes. Take off the heat and puree in a blender or use an immersion blender to smooth out the curry. Place back in the pan and cook to thicken the curry, if it seems a bit thin. Add the eggs and continue to cook for another 5 minutes.

Sides and Garnishes

Sides and garnishes come in endless variations. Egg curry is typically garnished with cilantro and slices of lime and served over plain rice and/or with *naan* or *raiti* (Indian flatbread) on the side.

Raita is made with yogurt infused with fresh mint and flavored with spices like coriander and a bit of spicy chile powder. Bananas can be sliced lengthwise, then fried in a pan with butter or ghee and brown sugar; set aside and serve at room temperature. A sautéed onion topping can also be made ahead of time. In a pan with a tablespoon or so of oil, add a few spices like coriander seed, black mustard seed, cumin seed and a pinch of turmeric. Slice a large onion (or two) into very thin rings. Sauté them in a pan with the spices and set aside to serve as a topping for the curry.

Some sides that need no preparation are golden raisins, small chopped up bits of dried mango, shredded coconut, raw or roasted almonds or cashews, and a variety of chutneys. Roasted almonds or cashews can be easily and quickly made by roasting raw nuts with a small bit of oil in a small cast iron pan, then salting them. Serve after cooling them a bit.

Kofta

Kofta is a spiced meatball. The word has Urdu and Persian origins and means "pounded meat." Kofta is a family of meatball or meatloaf dishes found in Middle Eastern and Indian cooking. Instead of a Western spaghetti meal of meatballs in sauce served over noodles, the Eastern take is meatballs in a curry served over rice.

The Kofta mince combines meat (beef, chicken, lamb or mutton) with spices in varying combinations. Eastern versions are more likely to contain lamb or mutton, but westernized versions more often use beef. This version from my sister-in-law, Kiran, is gentler on the spices, to cater to the western palate.

Kiran's Kofta

Serves 6 to 8

Meatballs

1/2 onion, roughly chopped
2 cloves garlic, roughly chopped
1-inch ginger, roughly chopped
1/2 serrano pepper, roughly chopped, or 1 teaspoon red pepper powder
1 pound fatty (80/20) ground beef or lamb
1 teaspoon salt
1 teaspoon coriander powder
1/2 teaspoon ground chiles
1/2 teaspoon turmeric
1 teaspoon garam masala, homemade or store-bought
1 egg
Handful of raisins
Handful of cashews, crushed
Oil for frying

Blend the onion, garlic cloves, ginger, and serrano pepper, if using, in a food processor. Add the ground meat, salt, coriander, ground chiles, turmeric, and garam masala and process until slightly pasty. Scrape meat mixture into a bowl and blend in the egg. Form into small meatballs, adding 1 raisin and the equivalent of 1 crushed cashew to the middle of each meatball when forming it into about 1-inch balls. Fry meatballs in a small amount of oil or bake in the oven, then drain. Set aside to cool and add to the curry later. The number of meatballs will vary with the cook's preparation, but the recipe should typically make 20 to 30 small meatballs.

Spices for the curry

1 teaspoon garam masala
1/2 teaspoon salt
1 teaspoon turmeric
1 teaspoon coriander powder
1/2 teaspoon paprika
1/4 teaspoon ground cardamom
1/4 teaspoon black pepper

Combine the spices in a bowl: the garam masala, salt, turmeric, coriander, paprika, cardamom and black pepper and set aside.

Curry

3 to 4 tablespoons cooking oil
1/4 teaspoon cumin seeds
1/2 teaspoon black mustard seeds
1 cinnamon stick
1 medium to large onion, sliced thinly, or chopped finely
3 tablespoons water, as needed
1-inch knob ginger, peeled or grated
2 cloves garlic, finely minced
1/2 to 1 whole green chile pepper, (Indian, Thai or serrano), chopped
1/4 teaspoon ground black pepper, ground
1 medium tomato, skin removed and pureed (about 1/2 cup)
1/3 to 1/2 cup plain yogurt
2 cups water
3 to 4 tablespoons heavy cream
Cilantro for garnish, optional

To make the curry, in a Dutch oven or large, heavy pan with deep sides, heat oil to a medium heat, then add cumin seeds and black mustard seeds. Once they begin to sputter and pop, add the cinnamon stick. Stir briefly, then add onions and cook for 10 minutes or so, until onions begin to brown.

Add 3 tablespoons of water to mix and continue to sauté for another 3 minutes. Add the ginger, garlic, green chiles and ground pepper, continue to sauté for a minute; then add the pureed tomato.

Transfer the reserved spice mix into the curry pot and cook for 5 to 6 minutes until thickened; then lower the heat. Stir a tablespoon or so of the masala into the yogurt, then add this yogurt blend to the pan. Sauté for another few minutes and add 2 cups of water. Bring to a boil and simmer for at least 5 minutes, cooking the curry down.

Add the koftas to the curry and cover the pot. Continue cooking over a low heat for 20 to 30 minutes. After it has finished cooking, and before serving, add a few tablespoons of heavy cream.

Garnish with cilantro and serve with naan (flatbread) or over basmati rice.

Kiran's Indian Pickle

The Indian pickle is known as "achar" in Hindi, and it is not like western-style pickles. Indian pickle tends to be savory, not sweet, and very hot with quantities of chile peppers. Pickle is portioned out in small quantities as a condiment. Mango, lemon, lime, cauliflower, carrots, and green beans are some of the fruits and vegetables used to create Indian pickle. Instead of fermenting in vinegar in western fashion, Indian pickle is fermented with oil, spices and salt.

It can be made as a fresh condiment or as preserved condiment to serve later. Many varieties can also be easily purchased at Asian markets.

My sister-in-law Kiran often offers Indian pickle on the table to accompany a curry meal, like the kofta mentioned above. Here is a fresh turmeric pickle that she makes. She reduced the amount of chiles in this recipe, for the western palate.

Haldi Ka Achar (Turmeric Pickle)

1 tablespoon black mustard seeds
1 heaping teaspoon cumin seeds
1 heaping teaspoon fennel seeds
1/2 teaspoon black peppercorns, whole
1/2 teaspoon ground cinnamon
2 teaspoons coriander seeds
6 to 8 mini carrots
1 to 2 green chiles, or a jalapeño for less heat, optional
Handful blanched string beans
1 1/2 to 2 cups fresh turmeric pieces, or twice the bulk of the carrots
1 to 2 tablespoons cooking oil
1/2 teaspoon asafoetida powder
1/4 teaspoon red chile powder
Few pinches salt
1 to 2 tablespoons lemon juice

Toast the spices (black mustard, cumin, fennel, black pepper, cinnamon and coriander) dry, in a small cast iron pan over low heat. Stir for a few minutes to toast them evenly, then remove them to another pan to cool.

Cut the carrots, string beans, and chiles or jalapeño into slices, lengthwise. Peel the turmeric and slice it into lengthwise pieces as well; combine all four in a bowl.

Take the cooled and toasted spices and grind in a spice grinder (or a dedicated coffee grinder) until coarsely ground.

In a deep-sided pan, heat the oil, then stir in the asafoetida. Add the carrot, string beans, chiles or jalapeño, and turmeric. Fry for a few seconds, then add the ground spice blend and 1/4 teaspoon red chile powder. Salt to taste and mix well. Pour over the lemon juice and mix well. Place in a serving dish and serve with your favorite curry.

References

I would like to thank my mother, Joyce Griffith and my sister-in-law, Kiran Griffith for their recipe recollections and turmeric information.

"7 British dishes inspired by Indian Cuisine." Times of India, https://timesofindia.indiatimes.com/life-style/food-news/7-british-dishes-inspired-by-indian-cuisine/articleshow/113097155.cms. Accessed 7-5-2025.

Brown, Mary-Eve, R.D.N., CS.O., L.D.N. "Turmeric Benefits." Johns Hopkins Medicine. https://www.hopkinsmedicine.org/health/wellness-and-prevention/turmeric-benefits. Accessed 7-5-2025.

Claproth, Gwenna. "What is Rijsttafel? A Dish to Bridge Dutch and Indonesian Identities." Smithsonian Center for Folklife & Cultural Heritage Magazine. https://folklife.si.edu/magazine/rijsttafel-dutch-indonesian-identities#. Accessed 7-7-2025.

"Dutch East India Company." Britannica. https://www.britannica.com/topic/Dutch-East-India-Company. Accessed 7-20-2025.

"Dutch-Indonesian Food: A Culinary Colonial Legacy." Expatica. https://www.expatica.com/nl/lifestyle/food-drink/dutch-indonesian-food-505212/. Accessed 7-7-2025.

Martins, Kim. "Dutch East India Company." World History Encyclopedia. https://www.worldhistory.org/Dutch_East_India_Company/. Accessed 7-20-2025.

Masters, Maria. "10 Proven Health Benefits of Turmeric Spice and Roots." Prevention. https://www.prevention.com/food-nutrition/healthy-eating/a20635784/turmeric-benefits/?utm_source=google&utm_. Accessed 7-20-2025.

Prasad, Sahdeo, and Aggarwal, Bharat B. "Chapter 13 Turmeric, the Golden Spice: From Traditional Medicine to Modern Medicine." NIH National Library of Medicine, National Center for Biotechnology Information. https://www.ncbi.nlm.nih.gov/books/NBK92752/. Accessed 7-7- 2025.

"Rijsttafel." Wikipedia. https://en.wikipedia.org/wiki/Rijsttafel. Accessed 7-7-2025.

Skye Suter has been involved with art and plants for most of her life. She worked at a newspaper as an Art Director and wrote garden and food columns. Skye worked at a botanical garden and for other non-profits in marketing and producing graphic design, as well as educational programming.

She is a member of the International Herb Association, where she formerly served on the IHA Board, and is a member of the Herb Society of America. Locally, she is a member of PPSEAWA New York and the Staten Island Herb Society, as well as a past president. She is on the Board of Friends of Blue Heron Park, Inc. where she enjoys walking the trails and guiding plant-related programming.

Currently she is a freelance writer, occasional illustrator and graphic designer. Her disciplines are showcased through the work she does for organizations that reflect her interests in plants, nature, art, crafting, cooking and especially herbs. Skye can be reached at skyesuter@gmail.com.

The lime bath and the pickles' crunchy texture are the source of the "concrete" pickle name. *Chuck Voigt*

My Favorite Sweet Pickle Recipe

Chuck Voigt

Sometime in the very late 1950s or early 1960s, this pickle recipe came to my mother, possibly through her good friend, Florence Buckman. As can be seen in the recipe, these are not low-sugar pickles, but they are the best-tasting ones I have found. They have ruined me for any other sweet pickle. Don't eat too many at a time if you are sensitive about sugar.

The 24-hour lime soak removes any bitter taste from the cucumbers but also ensures a good snappy crunch. This lime bath and the pickles' crunchy texture are the source of the "concrete" pickle name.

The small number of ingredients is amazing, given the big flavor of the finished product. The two key spices are turmeric and celery seed. I think Florence might have liked adding just a dash of cloves to hers, which ruins them for me, but suit yourself.

They are good with almost anything, or just by themselves. Although it is not the first thing you might think about to enhance a slice of pizza, the two seem to mutually improve each other, at least for me.

Give them a try but be prepared to love them above all others. Enjoy!

Concrete Pickles

1 gallon, thickly-sliced, skin-on cucumbers (we did 5 quarts)
2 cups pickling lime

Cover cucumbers with water in a crock, enamel pan, or other non-metal container. Add and mix in lime. Let stand 24 hours. Pour off limey water where it won't cause problems (gravel driveway). Rinse with clear water 3 times. After third rinse, water should be clear when poured off.

Cover with ice water and let stand 3 hours. Drain.

To mix pickling liquid:

2 quarts white vinegar
3 teaspoons salt
8 cups sugar
1 tablespoon ground turmeric
3 tablespoons celery seed

In a large stainless or enamel pan, pour mixture over cucumbers; let stand in pickling liquid overnight.

The following morning, bring the contents of the pan to a boil and boil for 30 minutes, stirring occasionally.

Pack into clean, sealable jars immediately. Allow to seal as they cool.

You can save any leftover juice for adding to the next batch, or it works well for pickling beets.

Charles Voigt is a retired faculty member at the University of Illinois at Urbana-Champaign. He was a state vegetable and herb specialist there from 1988 through 2015. In 1989, he was on the steering committee that wrote the bylaws forming the Illinois Herb Association. He first presented a talk at the International Herb Growers and Marketers Association (later renamed International Herb Association or IHA) in 1991. He was head of the host committee for IHA's 1995 conference in Chicago, IL, and again in 2010 for the conference in Collinsville, IL. At the Portland, OR, IHA conference in 2001 he received IHA's Service award, and in 2010, in Collinsville, IL, their Professional Award. In 2014 in Toronto, he presented the Otto Richter Memorial Lecture at the annual IHA conference. He served on the IHA Program Committee for many years and has been the chair of the Horticulture Committee since 1997. This committee has been instrumental in choosing and promoting Herbs of the Year. Chuck is currently the chair of the IHA Foundation, as well. He also wrote the popular book, *Vegetable Gardening in the Midwest*, with his vegetable mentor, Dr. Joseph Vandemark. One of Chuck's goals in retirement is to sing in 100 gardens, although the pandemic of 2020 put a crimp in that process, and he's stalled at seventeen.

essential flavor
in pickles, mustard, curry
kitchen alchemy

Susan Belsinger

Turmeric

Curcuma longa

Turmeric is native to tropical South Asia and its
bright yellow rhizome has been used
medicinally since ancient times.
The spice is basic to many East Indian, Persian,
and Thai dishes.
First used in America as a dye and pickling
spice, today turmeric is recognized for its
powerful anti-inflammatory properties.

Ozark Folk Center State Park
Heritage Herb Garden

Turmeric for Health & Beauty

Ingredients for making turmeric bitters. *Susan Belsinger*

Mellow Yellow Bitters with Turmeric & Ginger

Susan Belsinger

These digestive bitters have stomach-soothing properties. They are bitter from the dandelion, gentian and turmeric, yet they have aromatic properties from the complementary fragrant spices.

Makes about 1 generous cup

Generous 1 tablespoon freshly grated turmeric root, or 1 teaspoon dried, ground turmeric
Generous 1 tablespoon freshly grated gingerroot, or 1 teaspoon dried, ground ginger
1 teaspoon dandelion root, coarsely ground
1/2 teaspoon gentian root
1/2 teaspoon decorticated (outer shells removed) cardamom seeds, coarsely ground
1/2 teaspoon toasted fenugreek seeds, coarsely ground
1/4 teaspoon fennel seeds, coarsely ground
1/8 teaspoon black peppercorns, coarsely ground
1 cup 100-proof vodka
1/2 cup water
2 to 3 teaspoons local honey, pure maple syrup or organic sugar

Combine the prepared herbs, seeds and roots in a pint jar or bottle. Pour the alcohol over the botanicals to fill the jar and completely cover them. Cap the bottle or jar, label and date, and shake the container daily for 2 weeks. Open and taste the bitters. If you are happy with the strength and flavor, strain the menstruum from the marc; if you want it to be a bit stronger, leave the botanicals in the menstruum and wait another week or two.

After straining the bitters, put them aside and put the marc into a small saucepan and cover with 1/2 cup water and bring to a simmer. Simmer gently for 10 minutes, checking that there is still liquid in the pan. Place a lid on the pan and let cool a bit; while still warm stir in 2 teaspoons sweetener. Strain the liquid from the marc and add it to the bitters; discard the marc to the compost. Bottle the bitters, preferably in a dark glass bottle with a dropper, and label. Store in a cool dark place away from direct sunlight. Take a half dropperful about 1/2 hour before or after meals.

Blue Turmeric

I've found that blue turmeric (*Curcuma aeruginosa*) is much more bitter in flavor than *C. longa*—so it would be great to use in making bitters—it is so bitter that I would probably leave the bittering agent gentian root out if using blue turmeric rhizomes.

Little did I know what a can of worms I was opening when trying to figure out the difference between *Curcuma caesia* versus *Curcuma aeruginosa*, both referred to as blue turmeric and sometimes black turmeric. There was not much definitive information in the first 10 to 15 resources that I went to. In fact, of the 93 species of *Curcuma*, there is a lot of confusion and controversy. I had already discussed this subject with Henry Flowers, a professional gardener/ herbalist friend who grows many types of Zingiberaceae in his Texas gardens. We both agreed on confusion in identifying the two species—and believed that the *C. caesia* rhizomes that we started with seemed to be more likely *C. aeruginosa*.

I am citing the following source for information that I have deciphered below: "Jose S, Thomas TD. Comparative phytochemical and anti-bacterial studies of two indigenous medicinal plants *Curcuma caesia* Roxb. and *Curcuma aeruginosa* Roxb." *International Journal of Green Pharmacy* 2014;8:65-71. The original study was carried out with the objective to investigate the phytochemical and anti-bacterial activity of two folklore medicinal plants, *C. caesia* and *C. aeruginosa*.

"*Curcuma caesia* commonly known as 'Black turmeric' is a perennial underutilized herb of the family Zingiberaceae. The plant is mainly distributed in the Himalayan region, north-east and central India. It usually grows well in moist deciduous forests." The plant rhizome is described as having bluish-black colored flesh with a pungent smell and hot bitter taste. "The characteristic pungent smell of the rhizome is due to the presence of essential oil rich in camphor and starch. Due to its high medicinal value, the plant is in great demand in central India."

"*C. aeruginosa* is a native tropical plant of Southeast Asia, including Myanmar, Cambodia, Vietnam, Malaysia, Indonesia and Thailand and Western Ghats of south India." Its greenish-blue rhizomes, have a mild aroma reminiscent of ginger. The International Union for Conservation of Nature reports that this plant is considered critically endangered due to its many medical virtues and overharvesting from the wild.

The findings from this study are that these two turmerics are morphologically similar indigenous plants with various levels of anti-bacterial activity. Both *C. caesia* and *C. aeruginosa* have rhizomes with pungent aroma, bitter taste and medicinal value. Other similarities are flower spikes with purple calyces and purple-brown midribs. *C. caesia* has a central, dark pink flower spike, a purple-brown leaf sheath and the color of the rhizome is dark blue, while *C. aeruginosa* has a central/lateral light pink flower spike, a dark purple leaf sheath and a greenish-blue rhizome. Grow them for the experience, their beauty, and their bitter medicine.

The very bitter blue turmeric rhizome, *Curcuma aeruginosa*, is valued for its many medicinal properties. *Susan Belsinger*

Elderberry Fire Cider ingredients in apple cider vinegar, ready to macerate; shake daily. *Susan Belsinger*

Elderberry & Fire Cider Elixir with Fresh Turmeric

Susan Belsinger

This is one of my favorite versions of fire cider that I make. You can slice the horseradish, gingerroot and turmeric into coins—or grate them. The flavors will be stronger if the roots/rhizomes are grated. I've been making fire cider ever since I apprenticed with Rosemary Gladstar over 20 years ago. There are probably as many variations of this recipe as there are herbalists. Every year, I get together with my Sage Sisters and we make fire cider together— each one of us bringing an ingredient—our own jars and acv. This recipe is adapted from my recipe for Elderberry Fire Cider Elixir in Fire Cider! by Rosemary Gladstar & Friends.

flavortherapy

▶ This elixir slams the tastebuds and is very stimulating. It is warming and usually causes me to break out in an immediate sweat.

Makes about 2 quarts

About 1/2 cup grated horseradish root
About 1/2 cup grated gingerroot
About 1/2 cup grated turmeric root
1 small bulb garlic or about 3 tablespoons chopped garlic
Scant 1 cup chopped onion
1 or 2 fresh or dried chiles, chopped or 1 teaspoon ground cayenne pepper
8 or 10 black peppercorns
Scant 1/2 cup dried elderberries or about 1 cup fresh or frozen elderberries
1 fresh lemon or orange, halved lengthwise and sliced crosswise
About 1 1/2 quarts organic apple cider vinegar
1/2 to 1 cup honey, preferably raw and local

To make fire cider, thinly slice or grate the horseradish, ginger and turmeric roots, chop the garlic and onion and mince the chile peppers. I don't really measure—just sort of follow the recipe loosely—I usually double the recipe so there is plenty for the family and some to share.

Divide the ingredients into two 1-quart jars and add apple cider vinegar to a few inches above the ingredients. Cover tightly with a non-metallic lid and shake well. Label and date jar.

Try to remember to shake it daily and let it infuse for anywhere from 4 to 8 weeks—though if necessary, I use it even after just 24 hours of infusion. If you leave it to macerate for longer, it has a predominant allium flavor, so it is best to strain it off before it gets too potent.

Strain through cheesecloth or muslin to remove the herbal marc (chickens love the leftover botanical marc and so does the compost pile).

Taste and add honey; start with the lesser amount, taste and add more if desired. Some folks like to add a little bit of honey—others like to add a lot to make it more palatable (which also is great for coughs or a scratchy throat).

Pour into clean, bottles or jars (dark glass if you have them), seal with a non-metallic lid, label and store out of sunlight. Keep out of reach of children.

creative possibilities

▶ I like using fresh chiles like fatali, lemon drop or cayenne.

▶ Some herbalists add rosemary, thyme, sage or other herbs.

▶ Elderberries add their immunostimulant virtues—if you don't have them make the fire cider anyway.

▶ I take a spoonful every day. When I'm feeling cold, sore throat or flu symptoms, I take it by the shot glass a few times a day—sipping slowly and letting it mix with saliva before swallowing.

This infusion of power-packed botanicals macerated in apple cider vinegar and sweetened with honey really is a go-to preventative and remedy for herbalists around the globe—it works on colds, flu and sore throat. *Susan Belsinger*

Prepping the ingredients with Sage Sisters to make fire cider makes the task fun and light, and the end result is full of the best ingredients and healing energy. *Susan Belsinger*

Fresh grated turmeric makes a much tastier beverage, although good-quality powdered turmeric is perfectly fine. *Susan Belsinger*

50 Years of Golden Milk

Susan Belsinger

I first drank golden milk while studying Kundalini yoga in an Ashram in 1971. They drank this age-old Ayurvedic beverage every night before going to bed and said that it "oiled the joints and kept us limber." Powdered turmeric turned the milk golden yellow in color and we all know that warm milk is supposed to help us sleep. (Besides being high in antioxidants, present day studies have shown that it reduces joint pain and inflammation— see https://www.healthline.com/nutrition/golden-milk-turmeric#section9 for "10 healthful reasons to drink golden milk.")

The concoction seemed strange to me at first, however once you drink it a few times, it becomes a pleasant beverage. Of course, fresh grated turmeric makes a much tastier beverage, although good-quality powdered turmeric is perfectly fine. The black pepper is an essential ingredient; the piperine in the pepper helps the body to better absorb the curcumin in the turmeric, as does the fat.

Back in the ashram days, it was ghee and honey with the turmeric and pepper—nowadays there are many versions of golden milk—and actually I prefer the coconut oil and maple syrup combo with organic whole milk, cashew or oat milk.

I've seen jars of the golden milk mix with all sorts of other ingredients added (see creative possibilities below), for sale at health food stores and drugstores (it is very spendy)—with labels that say just add milk. Making your own is much less costly. This recipe makes 1 cup; just multiply the recipe for however many people you are serving.

flavortherapy

▶ Grounding, relaxing & balancing—I can drink this before bed and fall asleep.

▶ Simple and nourishing; turmeric has an earthy taste.

Makes 1 serving

1 cup milk—your choice of dairy or plant-based
1 tablespoon fresh, finely grated turmeric root or 1 teaspoon ground turmeric
1 teaspoon ghee, unsalted butter or coconut oil
1 to 2 teaspoons local honey or pure maple syrup
About 2 grinds black pepper (or 1 pinch)

Heat the milk in a small, heavy-bottomed saucepan. As it warms, add the turmeric, fat, sweetener and black pepper and stir well with a small whisk to combine. Once hot, stir, turn off the heat and put a saucer or lid on the pan and let it sit for 5 minutes or so before serving (steeping seems to meld the flavors together more). Taste and adjust seasonings if need be.

Pour into a mug and serve hot. (If using fresh turmeric root, you may want to strain the golden milk into your mug.) Stir before serving.

creative possibilities

▶ Use any type of milk: organic whole milk, 2% or nonfat, coconut milk, cashew, almond, soy or oat milk.

▶ Variations include additions of ground or fresh grated ginger (which is a stimulant), ground cinnamon and/or powdered ashwaganda and/or astragalus root, vanilla extract or powder, cardamom, fennel, mace or nutmeg, star anise or any spice or herb that you'd like to add.

▶ Use whatever sweetener you prefer: I like maple syrup best, then honey—there is also sorghum syrup (strong in flavor) and agave, organic sugar, or some use stevia.

▶ Although ghee was the traditional fat, butter or coconut oil work just as well—in fact I prefer the flavor of the coconut oil.

▶ My friend Tina Marie Wilcox adds semi-sweet chocolate chips to her golden milk.

Natural Beauty with Turmeric

Janice Cox

Turmeric has become a superstar in the world of wellness, showing up in everything from golden lattes to healing skin balms. Its popularity is at an all-time high, and everyone is in love with this vibrant yellow-orange spice. But turmeric is anything but new. In fact, it has been used for centuries as both a healing remedy and a cosmetic ingredient.

When it comes to body care, turmeric offers a wide range of benefits—from promoting glowing skin and aiding in healing to treating acne and boosting circulation. These benefits are due to its high content of curcumin, a powerful anti-inflammatory and antioxidant compound. Studies have shown that turmeric supports skin healing by reducing inflammation and oxidative stress. It also has a positive effect on tissue repair and collagen production.

This is why turmeric is increasingly featured in commercial cosmetic products—and why it remains a staple in Ayurvedic beauty practices. Below are a few natural beauty recipes that highlight this beloved root. Enjoy!

Ayurveda

Ayurveda is a holistic health practice that originated in India over 3,000 years ago. The word Ayurveda means "the science of life." This natural approach to wellness focuses on supporting balance in the body, mind, and spirit. It is based on the belief that all aspects of the body are interconnected—when one area is out of balance, it can affect the others. Thanks to its powerful health benefits, turmeric is commonly used in both Ayurvedic nutrition and body care treatments.

Golden Milk Cleanser mask is both cleansing and moisturizing. *Janice Cox*

Glowing Facial Mask

Note: Before applying turmeric to your face, always perform a patch test and wait 24 hours to see how your skin reacts. While turmeric can be used on its own, it may leave a slight yellow tint on the skin. That is why it is best to mix it with other natural ingredients.

In this recipe, honey is added for its skin-healing and antibacterial properties—it helps keep your skin clean, clear, and glowing. You can find turmeric powder or ground turmeric in the spice section of most grocery stores.

Yields 1 ounce

1 teaspoon ground turmeric powder
1 teaspoon raw honey
2 tablespoons water

In a small bowl, stir together all ingredients until smooth and well blended.

To use, apply the mask to clean skin using a small brush or cotton pad. Let it sit for 10 minutes, then rinse thoroughly with warm water. Gently pat your skin dry.

Golden Milk Cleanser

Drinking turmeric milk—also known as "golden milk"—is well known for supporting overall health and boosting the immune system. If you are feeling under the weather, a warm cup before bed may help soothe and restore you.

This same golden milk can also be used as a gentle, nourishing skin cleanser. It is both cleansing and moisturizing, making it ideal for all skin types— especially sensitive or mature skin.

Yields 8 ounces

1 cup whole milk (or substitute with coconut milk)
1 teaspoon ground turmeric powder

In a small saucepan, combine the milk and turmeric powder. Warm gently over low heat, stirring well—do not boil. Let the mixture cool completely.

To use, massage the golden milk into damp skin and let it sit for 1 to 2 minutes. Rinse thoroughly with cool water and gently pat your skin dry.

Store any leftover cleanser in a covered container in the refrigerator. It will keep for up to two weeks.

Troubled Skin Toner

Turmeric is considered a super spice—especially when it comes to treating acne and troubled skin. Its natural antiseptic and anti-inflammatory properties help fight bacteria and prevent it from spreading. Turmeric also promotes healing and helps reduce redness and irritation caused by blemishes.

Keeping your skin clean and balanced is essential for a healthy complexion. If you cannot find fresh turmeric at your grocery store, you can substitute powdered turmeric root or even turmeric tea in this recipe.

Yields 8 ounces

1 cup boiling water
6 slices fresh turmeric root, sliced into coins

Place the turmeric slices in a small bowl or heat-safe container. Pour the boiling water over the turmeric and allow the mixture to cool completely. Strain out the turmeric and pour the liquid into a clean container with a tight-fitting lid.

To use, after cleansing your face, apply the toner using a cotton pad or a fine mist spray bottle. Let it absorb into your skin—do not rinse.

Turmeric Pads for Puffy Eyes

A classic remedy for dark circles and puffiness is a cold compress—but you can boost its power with turmeric. This golden spice has natural lightening and anti-inflammatory properties that help reduce the appearance of under-eye circles and stimulate circulation to minimize puffiness.

Keep a jar of these cooling pads in your freezer and use them whenever needed—after a late night or too much screen time. You can also use these cool pads to calm a sunburn or soothe a bug bite.

Yields approximately 8 ounces (about 12 pads)

1 to 2 turmeric tea bags
1 cup boiling water
1 teaspoon aloe vera gel

Place the turmeric tea bags in a small bowl and pour the boiling water over them. Let the mixture steep and cool completely. Remove the tea bags and stir in the aloe vera gel.

Soak two half-circle cotton pads (cut cosmetic rounds in half) in the solution. Lay the soaked pads on parchment paper on a small tray. Freeze until very cold or solid. To store, make several at once and store them in a resealable container or bag in the freezer for easy use.

To use, place two frozen pads under your eyes and leave on for 5 to 10 minutes. Relax and enjoy the soothing effects.

Hydrating Body Butter

You can infuse your favorite skin oils with turmeric and use them in recipes for soothing balms and creams. When creating infused oils, always use dried turmeric—never fresh—to avoid introducing moisture, which can lead to bacterial growth and spoilage.

This simple body butter is easy to make and perfect for dry, rough areas that need extra care and protection. Coconut oil adds rich moisture and is known for its calming, skin-soothing properties.

Yields 4 ounces

1 tablespoon dried turmeric root or powder
1/2 cup coconut oil
1 tablespoon cocoa butter or shea butter

Place all ingredients in a small saucepan and gently heat on the stovetop until the oil and butter just begins to melt. Remove from the heat and stir until well mixed. Let cool completely and let sit for a few days. Gently reheat the mixture and strain out all solids before pouring into a clean container. Keep stored in a covered container in the refrigerator for up to several months. To use, massage into your skin.

Haldi Wedding Paste

Haldi is a cherished pre-wedding ritual in Hindu tradition, where family and friends apply a paste made of turmeric and other natural ingredients to the bride and groom's skin. Accompanied by joyful songs and chanting, the ceremony is a time of celebration, love, and bonding. The turmeric paste is believed to bless the couple and purify their bodies and minds as they prepare for their new life together.

This Haldi-inspired body mask blends ground oats and rosewater with turmeric to create a nourishing treatment that promotes radiant, glowing skin.

Yields approximately 8 ounces

1 cup whole or rolled oats
1 tablespoon dried turmeric
1 tablespoon dried rose petals
1 tablespoon rosewater

In a food processor combine the oats, turmeric and rose petals and process until the mixture resembles whole grain flour. Pour the mixture into a jar or bowl. Stir in the rosewater.

To use, massage the mixture into damp skin in a circular motion. Let sit for 15 minutes, then rinse with lukewarm water in the bath or shower. Store leftover paste in a covered container in the refrigerator.

Janice's herbal girl tradition continues with the Turmeric Girl. *Janice Cox*

Curcuma longa. Köhlers Medizinal Pflanzen, 1890. *plantillustrations.org*

The Medicinal Uses of Turmeric (*Curcuma longa*)

Daniel Gagnon

Turmeric (*Curcuma longa* L.) [*Zingiberaceae*] (Zimmermann 2023)

Synonyms: *Curcuma domestica* VAL (Zimmermann 2023)

Other Common Names
Ayurvedic: Sanskrit: Haridra (literally means "yellow") (Gogte 2017) **Chinese Pinyin:** Jiang huang (rhizome) (Zimmermann 2023). **Dutch:** Kurkuma, curcuma (Van Hellemont 1986). **English**: Common turmeric, Indian saffron, yellow ginger (Zimmermann 2023), long rooted curcuma (Teuscher 2005). **French**: Safran des Indes, turméric, souchet de l'Inde, arrow-root de l'Inde (Teuscher 2005), rhizome de curcuma (Wichtl 2004). **German**: Kurkuma, gelbwurz, glebwurzelstock, Indischer safran, safranwurzel, langer gelbwurzelstock, turmerik gelber Ingwer (Teuscher 2005). **Hindi:** Haldi (Pole 2006). **Japanese:** Ukon (Witchtl 2004). **Javanese**: temo lavak (Weiss 1988). **Nepalese:** Haku halu (Kapoor 2001). **Persian:** Zardchob (Kapoor 2001). **Spanish**: Rizoma de cúrcuma, azafrán de la India (Wichtl 2004). **Tamil**: Manjal (Kapoor 2001). **Unani**: Haldi (Kapoor 2001)

Part Used

The rhizomes (Wichtl 2004). They are commonly referred to as roots. Turmeric rhizomes have a deep yellow to orange pulp and consist of two distinct parts. The mother rhizome is egg-shaped and is an extension of the plant's stem. The secondary rhizomes (called fingers) are of two types. The first types are long, cylindrical, branched parts that grow downwards from the "mother" rhizome. The second types are shorter and fatter (Chitra 2016, Yen 1992). The rhizomes grow for approximately 9 months and are ready to be harvested in the fall, or through January, as the leaves of the plant yellow and wither. When used fresh, the rhizomes are washed and peeled just before being used. When prepared as dried rhizomes, they are dug up, cleaned, steamed or boiled, and dried (Evans 1989). In the past, turmeric was used as an adulterant to ginger and mustard (Uphof 1968).

Key Constituents

Fresh turmeric rhizomes contain protein (6.3%), fat (5.1%), minerals (3.5%), carbohydrates (40-69%) and moisture (13.1%). They contain between 0.3 to 7.2% (generally between 4 to 5 %) yellow to orange lipophilic phenolic pigments known as curcuminoids or diarylheptanoids. These compounds include curcumin (diferuloylmethane) (~75%), desmethoxycurcumin (~10-20%), bisdemethoxycurcumin (~5%), p-coumaroylferuloylmethane, curcumenone, and curlone. The essential oil (3-5%) contains about 60% turmerone, 25% zingiberene as well as ar-turmerone, α-turmerone, and β-turmerone. Minor amounts of essential oil constituents include 1,8 cineole, germacrone, β-bisabolene, α-phellandrene, δ-sabinene, and borneol. Sugars found in the rhizomes are composed of glucose (2%), fructose (12%), arabinose (1%), and the glycans ukonan A, B, C and D. Other constituents include fixed oil; vitamins (especially vitamin C); resins; and others. Additionally, gelatinized starch (v~40%) is found in the rhizomes. The constituent curcumin is soluble in ethanol, alkali, ketone, acetic acid, and chloroform (Bone 2013, Chattopadhyay 2004, Duke 1985 and 2002, Evans 1989 and 1996, Guenther, 1952, Jiang 2021, Leung 1996, Pengelly 2004, Wichtl 2004, Williamson 2002).

Difference between Turmeric Rhizomes and Curcuminoids/Curcumin

Throughout this monograph, you'll read information about either turmeric rhizome or a family of constituents extracted from the rhizomes called curcuminoids. The most abundant, better known, and most researched of the curcuminoids is curcumin. Curcumin is the constituent that is most favored in clinical trials. It is also the one most readily available as a dietary supplement. Even though curcumin is derived from turmeric rhizomes, it is often used differently than the turmeric rhizome powder. The rhizomes are the "roots" of the turmeric plant that have been dried and powdered. They contain curcuminoids, including curcumin, but at a low percentage. The average concentration of naturally occurring curcuminoids in turmeric rhizomes hovers at around 2 to 7%, depending on the plant variety, growing region, and growing conditions. On the other hand, curcuminoids extracted from the turmeric rhizomes may be concentrated up to 95 to 100% of the resulting powder. To give a better understanding of the difference between the two products, let me use an analogy. Consider the differences between an orange and a vitamin C tablet. An orange contains water, fiber, bioflavonoids, proteins, vitamins, minerals, and many other constituents, as well as between 30 to 100 mg of Vitamin C. A vitamin C tablet may contain 500 mg of this vitamin and no other constituents. The orange is the sum of many constituents while vitamin C is a single constituent. The same thing goes for turmeric rhizome power and curcuminoids/curcumin.

Herbal Properties

Turmeric possesses a profusion of medicinal properties. These include alterative, amebicide, analgesic (NSAID-like effect, by inhibiting biosynthesis of prostaglandins), anaphrodisiac, anorectic, anthelmintic, antiaflatoxin, antiaggregant, antiallergic, antiarthritic, antibacterial, anticancer, antiedemic, antifungal, antihistamine, **anti-inflammatory** (by inhibiting cyclooxygenases, which inhibit prostaglandins and thromboxanes, as well as lipoxygenases, which inhibit leukotrienes), antimicrobial, antimutagenic, antineoplastic, **antioxidant**, antiperiodic, antiplatelet, **antiproliferative**, antiprotozoal, antirheumatic, antiseptic, antispasmodic, antitumoral, antiulcer, antiviral, aromatic, astringent, bile stimulant, bitter tonic, blood purifier, cardioprotective, carminative, chemopreventive, cholagogue, choleretic, cholesterol reducing agent, cytotoxic, depurative, dermatological agent, detoxifier, digestive, diuretic, fibrinolytic, fungicide, gastroprotective, hepatoprotective, hypolipidemic, hypotensive, immunomodulant, immunostimulant, insecticide, laxative, nephroprotective, neuroprotective, ophthalmic, parasiticide, radioprotective, regenerator of liver tissue, sedative, stimulant, stomachic, tonic, uterotonic, vermifuge, vasoprotective, vasotonic alterative, and vulnerary properties. (Bartram 1998, Bone 2013, Duke 2002 and 2003, Menzies-Trull 2003, Pengelli 2004, Skenderi 2003, Wren 1988). These three herbal properties are highlighted here because most turmeric rhizome and curcumin clinical trials focus primarily on one of these three attributes.

General Description

Turmeric is a perennial herb that grows to approximately 1 meter high, belongs to the ginger family [*Zingiberaceae*], and is indigenous to tropical Southern Asia. Around 130 species of *Curcuma* have been identified. Some of the better-known include *Curcuma amada* (mango ginger), *C. aromatica* (wild turmeric), *C. kwangsiensis* (Guangxi turmeric), *C. phaeocaulis* (Curcuma phaeocaulis), *C. wenyujin* (Curcuma wenyujin), *C. zanthorrhiza* (Javanese turmeric), and *Curcuma zedoaria* (zedoary) (Zimmermann 2023). Two of these species, *C. longa* and *C. zanthorrhiza* are considered official herbal medicines in India (Bruneton 1987, Schaffner 1993).

Production of Turmeric

India is the #1 producer, consumer, and exporter of turmeric worldwide. The major cultivation areas are found in the states of Andrash Pradesh, Tamil Nadu, and Karnataka (Jadhav 2022). It is estimated that India produces about 80% of the world's turmeric and accounts for 60% of the world's export (Ganesan 2015, Turmeric Outlook 2025).

Two types of turmeric dominate the world market: Allepey and Madras. Both are named after their respective growing regions in India. Allepey turmeric has orange-yellow flesh and is predominant in the US market since American users prefer it as a spice and food colorant. In contrast, the Madras type is preferred by the British and Middle Eastern markets for its intense, brighter and lighter yellow color. The latter type is better suited for mustard paste, curry powder or paste used in oriental dishes (Jyotirmayee 2022). Turmeric is often used as an ingredient to color mustard. Many consumers expect a bright yellow mustard (e.g., French's Classic Mustard) and turmeric extracts provide the expected color to the product.

China, Myanmar, Nigeria, and Bangladesh are the next most significant producers and exporters of turmeric. It is also grown in Southeast Asian countries including Indonesia, Thailand, and the Philippines. Central America, Latin America, parts of Africa, and the Caribbeans further contribute to the world's turmeric supply (Jadhav 2022).

Turmeric and Curcumin: An Abridged History

The earliest turmeric reference known is found in the *Arthavaveda,* written approximately 4,000 years before the common era (BCE). It was used to "charm away jaundice" and was prescribed for the treatment of leprosy. For over 6,000 years, turmeric has been used as food, a spice, a coloring agent, and as a medicinal herb. Not just any medicinal herb! In the sub-continent of India, it was considered the *"Oushadhi,"* the most outstanding healing herb, the one above the rest (Jager, 1997). Turmeric was also mentioned in the *Yajnavalkiasamhita* around 2,000 years BCE (Ravindran 2007). It was listed in an Assyrian herbal dating from 600 years BCE (Cozmin 2024). It was mentioned by the Greek physician Dioscorides (ca. CE 40-90) (McCormick & Co, 1979). In 1280, Marco Polo described turmeric and marveled that it exhibited similar qualities to saffron. He noted that the herb grew in the Fujian region of China (Prasad 2011), in Sumatra, and along India's Malabar Coast (Nabhan 2014).

Turmeric plays a major role in the marriage rituals of India. Kumkum, also known as kumkumam, is a red powder used in India for religious and social markings. It is made from a combination of turmeric, slaked lime, and sometimes saffron. Kumkum is a significant part of Hindu women's identity. Its use at birth, before a wedding, and upon death is considered auspicious (Chin 1992). As part of an Indian pre-wedding ritual, a turmeric paste is applied to the bride and groom's face, hands, and feet. Its vibrant yellow color is considered good luck and symbolizes purity, protection, prosperity, and fertility in Indian culture (Caldecott 2006). In India turmeric is used in curries, in Japan it is served as a tea, in Thailand it is part of the composition of cosmetics, in China it is used as a dye, in Malaysia as an antiseptic, in Pakistan as an anti-inflammatory agent and in the United States it is found in mustard, cheese, butter and fries, both as a preservative and colorant (Hay 2019).

Until recently, in the United States, England, and France, turmeric was mainly recognized and used as a culinary spice. As I researched the herbal medicine literature for this paper, I found it interesting to note that turmeric was conspicuously absent from most Western herbal medicine books written prior to the early 1990s (Christopher 1976, Hoffmann 1983, Kloss 1975, Lust 1974, Mills 1991, Tyler 1993, Valnet 1992). Before that time, Western herbalism viewed turmeric as an antiquated herbal medicine. Maud Grieve, in her seminal book *A Modern Herbal* (1982) first published in 1931, barely devoted a paragraph to the usefulness of this herb. She wrote: "Turmeric is a mild aromatic stimulant seldom used in medicine except as a colouring. It was once a cure for jaundice." French MD and herbalist Henri Leclerc (1929) wrote that turmeric was used in India as a condiment/spice. He reported that "the natives use the rhizomes for their digestive properties and favorable action on the liver. Salves are used to treat skin inflammation."

Concurrently, in the 1980s, orthodox medicine underwent a significant shift in its understanding of inflammation. The scientific research shifted its attention from uncovering inflammation's traditional role as a response to infection or injury to a broader appreciation of its involvement in chronic diseases. This new perspective came from the recognition that even subtle, low levels of inflammation (below those associated with acute infections) contributed to the development of chronic conditions and diseases as well as cancer. The shift occurred simultaneously with the discovery of numerous inflammatory molecules and their binding sites. These discoveries shifted the understanding of inflammation from a purely protective response to a complex process. The awareness that inflammation could be present as an underlying condition for many individuals opened new avenues of research, diagnosis, and treatment strategies (Granger 2010).

The scientific discovery and validation of the anti-inflammatory and antioxidant properties of turmeric's curcuminoids started in India in the early 1970s (Arora 1971, Srimal 1971 & 1973). By the 1990s, research on the role of these compounds, especially curcumin, began to appear in scientific literature. In 1991, Michael Castleman (1991), a medicinal herb writer and early proponent of the healing properties of turmeric, was surprised that American herbalists were not paying attention to this herb. He wrote in his book *The Healing Herbs*: "Western herbalists, wake up. Turmeric is a healer." By the mid-1990s, studies, papers, and clinical trials focusing on inflammation began to appear in scientific journals. The power of turmeric and curcumin started making headlines. By 1990, there were less than 100 papers published on curcumin (Kunnunmakkara 2017). By 2014, researchers confirmed that over 6,000 papers had been published in the prior 20 years (Prasad 2014). By 2023, a research team found a staggering 6,000 published human clinical trials on the use of curcumin. Unlike the report by Prasad in 2014, their report did not include laboratory studies, in vitro tests, systematic reviews and meta-analyses (Panknin 2023). The published results of turmeric and curcumin highlight the positive effects of this herb and its constituents on chronic inflammation, oxidative stress, and many chronic diseases. Today, it is well documented that the antioxidant and anti-inflammatory properties of this herb and its constituents play a key role in the prevention and treatment of many acute and chronic inflammatory diseases (He 2015).

In the early 2000s, turmeric- and curcumin-based herbal supplements began their incursion into the marketplace. Their sales grew exponentially year after year. In the natural, health food, and specialty categories, sales skyrocketed from less than $2M in 2000 to $37M in 2023. Curcumin-based products went from not appearing on anyone's best seller lists to becoming the #1 best-selling dietary supplement of this channel in 2013. To this day, it remains in the top 3 positions.

In the mass market channel, curcumin-based products were the #3 best-seller dietary supplements in 2023 with sales of $137M. (Blumenthal 2014 and 2024). As science continues to discover and broaden its understanding of the powerful actions of turmeric/curcumin and their roles in diseases, they will continue to garner strong sales.

Here's a dizzying array of turmeric supplements to choose from—turmeric is in the top 3 herbal supplement sellers. *Susan Belsinger*

Medicinal Uses

Internally

Use for Alzheimer's disease, amyotrophic lateral sclerosis, arthritis, atherosclerosis, cancer (brain tumors, breast, cervical, chronic lymphocytic leukemia, colorectal, cutaneous T-cell lymphoma, gastric, head and neck squamous cell carcinoma, liver, lung, melanoma, multiple myeloma, pancreatic, osteosarcoma, ovarian, prostate, sarcoma, small cell and non-small cell lung, thyroid, and uterine), catarrhal cough, chest congestion, chronic anterior uveitis, common cold, depression, dysentery, dyspepsia, elevated blood lipids, eye disorders, fever, HIV-associated chronic diarrhea, hypercholesterolemia, inflammatory bowel disease (IBD), intermittent fever, irritable bowel syndrome, intestinal parasites, jaundice, liver cirrhosis, liver disorders, menstrual discomforts, metabolic syndrome, migraine, nonalcoholic fatty liver disease, osteoarthritis, polycystic ovarian syndrome, poor digestion, postoperative inflammation, precancerous lesions, premenstrual syndrome, psoriasis, rheumatoid arthritis, skin conditions, stomach ulcer, tropical pancreatitis, ulcerative colitis, and vomiting in pregnancy (Bone 2003 & 2013, Castleman 1991, Kapoor 2001).

In Traditional Chinese Medicine (TCM), turmeric is primarily used to break up blood stasis, move qi, promote menstruation, and relieve pain and swelling (Chen 2001, Yen 1992).

Externally

Arthritis, cancer, conjunctivitis, eczema, eye disorders, hemorrhoids, obstinate itching, parasitic skin diseases, ringworm, skin infections, sore eyes, sprains, ulcerative skin diseases, and wounds. In some Asian countries, the fresh rootstock juice is used externally for recent bruises, wounds and leech bites. A thin paste or coating of the powder is used in smallpox and chickenpox to speed up the scabbing process (Bone 2003 & 2013, Kapoor 2001, Uphoff 1968). *Note: turmeric stains the skin yellow.*

Turmeric's Health Benefits

Note: After reviewing hundreds of clinical trials, it appears that turmeric rhizome powder and curcumin do not cure many of the diseases or health challenges they are used against. However, because their medicinal actions are propelled by powerful antioxidant and anti-inflammatory properties, they soothe, settle, and resolve scores of health conditions and diseases that may seem disparate at first. When these conditions or diseases require the body to put out inflammation and remove large quantities of harmful free radicals, turmeric and curcumin should be considered as the first line of defense. Additionally, they are relatively inexpensive when compared to many drugs and have very few side effects, making them very useful as a support in inflammatory conditions of all types. Consider turmeric rhizomes or curcumin as strategic allies for whatever health issues you are dealing with. You can use them to either prevent these issues in the first place, prevent their relapses if you already are dealing with such issues, or to decrease the severity of the issues by decreasing the associated inflammation. It's really good stuff!

Eyes

Traditional Ayurvedic Medicine has recommended turmeric for eye problems for thousands of years (Pole 2006). To this day, in India, a wash made from turmeric rhizomes is used for eye afflictions such as conjunctivitis and styes (Frawley 2001). Turmeric is also used in Arabic medicine to treat eye infections. A paste of turmeric is applied around the eyes for three days (Ghazandar 1994). *Note: turmeric stains the skin yellow.*

Today, turmeric's active constituent, curcumin, has been shown to deliver its anti-inflammatory and antioxidant properties in eye conditions such as anterior uveitis, glaucoma, age-related macular degeneration (AMD), maculopathy, and diabetic retinopathy (DR) (Allegri 2010, Franzone 2021). Other common eye issues that are relieved by curcumin include dry eyes, conjunctivitis, pterygium, cataracts, and other corneal diseases (Liu 2017) as well as retinitis pigmentosa, central serous retinopathy, proliferative vitreoretinopathy, retinal ischemia reperfusion injury, and retinoblastoma (Chandrasekaran 2022). One of the major benefits of curcumin is that it downregulates the expression of many inflammatory genes, including IκBα, cyclooxygenase 2, prostaglandin E2, interleukin (IL)-1, IL-6, IL-8 and tumor necrosis factor-α, that contribute to and aggravates eye inflammation. When these genes are activated, inflammation ensues (Franzone 2021). Curcumin turns down the expression of these inflammatory genes, keeping inflammation at bay.

Studies have demonstrated curcumin's therapeutic role and efficacy in eye relapsing diseases, such as dry eye syndrome, allergic conjunctivitis, maculopathy, corneal neovascularization, ischemic retinopathy and diabetic retinopathy (Chen 2010, Pescosolido 2014, Radomska-Lesniewska 2019). Curcumin is used prophylactically to prevent these conditions from occurring in the first place (Chandrasekaran 2022). Research has shown that the effectiveness of curcumin following treatment is comparable to corticosteroid therapy. Additionally, when compared with corticosteroids, the lack of side effects from this natural substance is an undeniable advantage (Prasad 1999).

Mouth

Turmeric offers many benefits to support a healthy mouth. It has been used to reduce inflammation of the gums, burning mouth syndrome, oral mucositis especially during cancer treatment (see the cancer section), candidiasis, gingivitis, leukoplakia, canker sores, dentures and aphthous stomatitis (Indriyani 2025). Its antimicrobial properties combat bacteria and other oral microorganisms that contribute to inflammation of the oral cavity (Hussain 2022).

For periodontal issues such as gingivitis and periodontitis, herbalists suggest the use of turmeric paste as a topical application. To make the paste, mix 1 teaspoon of turmeric, 1/2 teaspoon salt, and 1/2 teaspoon of mustard oil together. Rub the teeth and gums with this paste twice daily. For dental pain and gum swelling, massage the aching tooth, teeth and/or gum with roasted, ground turmeric (Nagpal 2013).

Digestive Aid

In the Philippines, turmeric rhizome powder is used with coconut oil to stimulate or strengthen the digestive action of the stomach. In China, it is used for colic (Uphoff 1968). In Ayurvedic medicine, turmeric is used to promote a healthy metabolism in the body, correcting both deficiencies and excesses. It is thought to strengthen digestion, enhance the digestion of protein, and improve the health of the intestinal microbiome (Frawley 1996). It has been used to treat dyspepsia and stomach ulcers (both gastric and peptic ulcers). Turmeric increases the resistance of gastric mucosal cells to the damaging effects of strong irritants like hydrochloric acid. Turmeric supports the cellular integrity of gastric tissues and may be beneficial for the treatment of a variety of diseases in which stomach lining injuries are present (Prucksunand 1997). The anti-inflammatory properties and beneficial effects of curcumin have also been demonstrated for other gastrointestinal conditions including dyspepsia, *Helicobacter pylori* infection, and peptic ulcer (Hay 2019).

Turmeric is an excellent digestive bitter and carminative (an herb that stops the formation of gas and facilitates its expulsion). It is often added to foods including rice and bean dishes to improve digestion, reduce gas, and prevent bloating. Turmeric is recommended for people with chronic digestive weaknesses. It can be taken as a single liquid herbal extract or in the form of digestive bitters which combine turmeric with other bitter and carminative herbs. Turmeric is especially beneficial for people who feel tired after meals (Bhowmik 2009, Kuhn 2001).

Liver

In Western herbal medicine, turmeric is an important cholagogue. It is used to stimulate the production of bile. Enhanced bile production improves the body's ability to digest and absorb fats (Castleman 1991). Curcumin is currently being investigated as a treatment to prevent the progression of liver damage in different liver diseases. It is thought to do so by interfering with inflammation and fibrosis. Curcumin is a promising phytotherapy in chronic hepatitis and a potential therapeutic agent to reverse liver fibrosis and cirrhosis, especially when a hepatitis C virus infection is present (Buonomo 2019).

Intestines

Curcumin is indicated in inflammatory bowel disease (IBD) including Crohn's disease (CD) and ulcerative colitis (UC) (Mohseni 2025). It is also used in irritable bowel syndrome (IBS) (Hay 2019). Both UC and CD are chronic, debilitating, remitting, and relapsing inflammatory processes that occur due to a disruption in the immune response to intestinal microorganisms or other environmental conditions, leading to an imbalance between pro- and anti-inflammatory mediators (Goulart 2020). Studies have shown that curcumin leads to improvement in Crohn's inflammatory disease and even greater improvements in patients with ulcerative colitis. UC patients treated with curcumin showed a significant increase in clinical remission compared to the control group. Curcumin supplementation, when compared to placebo, demonstrates significant advantages in both clinical and endoscopic improvements (Peng 2025).

With its ability to modulate the gut microbiota, curcumin is a useful herbal tool in irritable bowel syndrome conditions (Ng 2018). Studies after studies show that curcumin is a safe and effective therapy for maintaining remission in ulcerative colitis when administered with standard drug treatments (Coelho 2020).

In addition to the high cost of conventional medications and the presence of numerous side effects in ulcerative colitis, a percentage of ulcerative colitis patients taking conventional drugs do not respond positively to the treatments. Although they do not benefit from taking corticosteroids and anti-TNF drugs, these patients respond positively to curcumin (Goulart 2020). Additionally, adults suffering from IBD who are supplemented with curcumin experience a 52% reduction in anxiety symptoms compared to a 16% reduction in the placebo group (Lopresti 2021).

In India, the juice from the rhizome is used as an anthelmintic (herb to get rid of parasitic worms) (Uphoff 1968). Curcumin has been used for intestinal parasites, specifically protozoans, thus explaining how it may be of use in dysentery (Castleman 1991). Curcumin also exerts an in vitro anti-parasitic effect against Trichomonas vaginalis, a protozoan that affects the human urogenital tract and causes trichomoniasis. Curcumin exerts an anti-inflammatory effect on the host, demonstrating the potential suitability of this constituent as a treatment for trichomoniasis (Mallo 2020).

Cancer

Curcumin is revealing itself to be a godsend in the fight against cancer. It is not a cure by any means. However, in many instances, it can play an important preventative role. It also has been shown to play a growing supportive role during the treatment of cancer. In many scientific circles, it is believed that most cancers are caused by disturbance in one or more of a multitude of gene expressions. This dysregulation leads to uncontrolled cell growth. Scientists are constantly looking for substances that target multiple gene products for the prevention and the treatment of this affliction. In the last 30 years, studies have shown that curcumin reduces cancer-related inflammation and may prevent cancer through various channels. Curcumin's lack of toxicity and broad-reaching mechanism of action is especially appealing. In addition, it is playing an increasingly important role as an adjuvant therapy, a therapy that is used after the initial cancer treatment to suppress secondary tumor formation. Many researchers suggest that curcumin should be used during and after chemotherapy, surgery, or radiation cancer treatments to decrease or prevent relapses (Wilken 2011).

In 2001, Cheng and colleagues performed a most impressive and important curcumin clinical trial against cancer. They conducted a clinical trial on five high-risk conditions: 1) recently surgically removed urinary bladder cancer; 2) Bowen's disease of the skin, a precancerous condition due to arsenic exposure; 3) uterine cervical intraepithelial neoplasm (CIN) (a.k.a.

cervical dysplasia); 4) oral leucoplakia, a precancerous mouth condition; and 5) intestinal metaplasia of the stomach, a precancerous stomach condition. They concluded that curcumin is beneficial in the prevention of cancer. They also demonstrated that curcumin is not toxic to humans in quantities up to 8,000 mg/day when taken orally for up to 3 months (Cheng 2001). This study literally changed the course of curcumin studies and its clinical trials in cancer treatments.

Hundreds of clinical trials featuring curcumin continue to highlight the supportive actions of curcumin against cancer. Here are curcumin's most important activities against cancer:

1. Curcumin inhibits numerous inflammatory molecules that may start, aggravate, or enhance the growth and metastasis of cancer. Inflammatory molecules such as cytokines, angiogenic factors, transcription factors, and enzymes are known to be involved with cancer development. This includes NF-κB (Nuclear factor kappa B), pro-inflammatory cytokines such as TNF-α, IL-6, IL-1β, and IL-23, cyclooxygenase-2 (COX-2), as well as matrix-degrading proteases that allow tumor cells to proliferate, invade and metastasize (Fan 2013).

2. Curcumin blocks carcinogenic substances that are encountered in every-day life such as tobacco smoke, vehicle emissions, ultraviolet radiation from the sun, pesticides, processed meat, radon, and air pollution. By blocking these and many other carcinogens, curcumin prevents these substances from causing cellular damage that may result in cancer. One critical way curcumin prevents cellular damage is by acting as a potent antioxidant that traps free radicals and renders them harmless (Lopez-Lazaro 2008).

3. Curcumin stops the invasion of tissues by substances called matrix metalloproteinases (MMPs). MMPs are involved in chronic diseases such as arthritis, Alzheimer's disease, psoriasis, chronic obstructive pulmonary disease, asthma, cancer, neuropathic pain, and atherosclerosis. The MMP family of enzymes play a crucial role in the breakdown and remodeling of extra cellular matrix (ECM). In short, ECM is a network of macromolecules that surround and support cells in tissues and organs. These breakdowns and remodeling in the targeted tissues may lead to unhealthy changes that facilitate tumor growth and cancer metastasis. The role of curcumin and MMPs in cancerous cell invasion, metastasis, and cancer progression has been studied extensively and the results show that curcumin prevents unhealthy changes in the remodeled tissues, protecting them from cancer (Wronski 2022).

4. Research has revealed that curcumin cuts off tumors' blood supply, a specialized network of blood vessels that feed tumors. By stopping or inhibiting the opportunity for tumors to create their own blood supplies, the abnormal clusters of cells are choked off, starved, and destroyed (Kunnumakkaran 2008).

5. Cells that become cancerous develop specific ways to evade programmed cell death, allowing these malignant cells to survive and accumulate. Curcumin enhances healthy apoptosis, the necessary destruction of older cells that are at the end point of their life cycle. Curcumin supports healthy cell life by ensuring that apoptosis is restored within the right survival time frame for each cell, and not beyond its actual healthy contribution and lifespan (Mortezaee 2019).

6. During the treatment of cancer, curcumin has been shown to improve the effectiveness of many cancer drugs. It also reduces the toxic effects of cancer drugs and radiotherapy on the body (Mansouri 2020, Kong 2021).

7. As a natural product, curcumin is non-toxic as well as wide-ranging in its ability to inhibit a multitude of unhealthy pathways involved in the formation of cancer and tumors in the body. While curcumin alone has shown some anti-tumor effects, its lack of systemic toxicity and broad-reaching mechanism of action make it ideally suited as a supportive therapy especially for cancers that are resistant to currently available therapies (Wilkens 2011).

8. Curcumin decreases the severity of cancer treatments' debilitating side effects. For example, a disabling side effect of breast cancer radiotherapy is radiation dermatitis which can range from mild redness to painful blistering, peeling, or even ulceration of the skin. Clinical trials confirm that curcumin is an effective substance that inhibits and controls radiation dermatitis in patients with breast cancer. Furthermore, it's been shown to improve the patients' overall clinical symptoms (Dahka 2023). Oral mucositis, an inflammation of the linings of the mouth is another debilitating side effect of cancer chemo and radiotherapy. In a clinical trial published in 2014, participants getting radiation treatments and using turmeric rhizome powder rinse saw a delay in the clinical appearance of mucositis. Additionally, the intolerable inflammation of the mouth linings was considerably reduced. Turmeric treatment was more effective than the povidone/iodine treatment that is normally used as the standard treatment (Rao 2014). See the How to Use Turmeric as Medicine section at the end of this paper for directions.

In a recent systematic review, scientists reviewed 22 clinical trials in cancer patients using curcumin. These trials confirmed that curcumin reduces the side effects of chemotherapy and radiotherapy, resulting in patients' improved quality of life. The studies also reported that curcumin increased patient survival time and decreased tumor markers' level. Furthermore, no specific toxic effects attributed to curcumin were reported in any of the 22 trials. The systematic review concluded that curcumin ought to be considered as a supplement in the therapeutic diets of cancer patients (Mansouri 2020). More recent reviews are echoing the same results, the same lack of side effects, and the same recommendation: Include curcumin in any cancer treatment plan.

Skin Inflammation, Itching, and Wound Healing

Curcumin has been investigated in several skin diseases including acne, alopecia, eczema, facial photoaging, oral lichen planus, premature skin aging, pruritus, psoriasis, radiodermatitis, skin inflammation, and vitiligo (Vaughn 2016). Curcumin is very useful in pruritus, a severe itching of the skin due to allergen contact, dry skin, pregnancy, dialysis, or as a reaction to some medications (Gogte 2017). Other skin conditions that respond positively to its use include facial redness and certain types of skin cancers. Oral supplementation of curcumin delivers therapeutic benefits for skin health with practically no adverse effects (Mata 2020). That's good news since it is well known that many of the drugs available for the treatment of chronic skin diseases, including glucocorticoids, can only be used for a limited amount of time, are of varying effectiveness, and often lead to adverse effects (Hengge 2006).

It is well known that diabetic patients often experience slow tissue repair and delayed wound healing. Curcumin used internally has been shown to stimulate skin wound repair in diabetic individuals (Sidhu 1999). It reduces wound healing times and improves collagen deposition, greatly helping in the first step of skin healing. Furthermore, it increases fibroblast and vascular density in wounds, the second step of skin healing (Kasprzak-Drozd 2024). Curcumin reduces the production of pro-inflammatory compounds and activates specific growth factors that stimulate skin healing. Clinical trials confirm the safety and efficacy of curcumin as a supplement for the prevention and treatment of skin diseases (Mohammadi 2024). In a study focusing on psoriasis, the researchers concluded that curcumin alone or in combination with conventional treatments effectively treated psoriasis (Zhang 2022). Curcumin provides protection against skin damage caused by prolonged exposure to UVB radiation.

Daniel Gagnon: "Over the last 30 years, one main area where turmeric and curcumin have made their names is in the arthritis arena." *Susan Belsinger*

End Stage Renal Disease (ESRD) is the final stage of chronic kidney disease. Patients at the ESRD stage often experience severe, debilitating itching. When patients took curcumin during a clinical trial, they reported a significant reduction in itching. No adverse reactions were observed (Pakfetrat 2014).

Cardiovascular Health

In Ayurvedic medicine, turmeric rhizome is used to stimulate blood formation, circulation, and act as a hemostatic, a substance that stops bleeding (Gogte 2017). Almost all the research on curcumin and the cardiovascular system has been done in the last 20 years. It has been investigated for its protective role in cardiovascular diseases including atherosclerosis, cardiac hypertrophy, myocardial infarction (heart attack), stroke, acute coronary syndrome, dyslipidemia, and heart failure (Fan 2013, Kumar 2021). Researchers believe curcumin may prevent cardiovascular disease through its ability to support the regulation of lipid metabolism. Its anti-atherogenic effect is due to its ability to decrease both high plasma (blood) cholesterol levels and free radical chains. Curcumin has a positive effect on serum triglyceride. Individuals taking curcumin notice a drop in their LDL and VLDL cholesterol levels. They also experience a positive change in the balance of "bad" LDL-cholesterol to "healthy" HDL-cholesterol (Alwi 2008, Hay 2019, Cox 2022). A recent study showed that curcumin could be used as a safe and well tolerated adjunct to statin drugs to control hyperlipidemia (Hay 2019).

Curcumin displays strong cardioprotective effects. These effects are primarily due to its well-known antioxidant and anti-inflammatory properties. Research shows that curcumin reduces risk of heart attacks in cardiac patients and plays a role in the prevention of some ventricular arrhythmias. It has also been shown to decrease myocardial injury that may occur after cardiac surgery (Wongcharoen 2009 & 2012). Other areas of research show that it may reduce the incidence of myocardial infarction (heart attack) as well as major negative cardiovascular events such as stroke, heart failure and cardiovascular deaths (Li 2023).

Joint Health

Over the last 30 years, one main area where turmeric and curcumin have made their names is in the arthritis arena. Arthritis is not a single condition. There are more than 100 forms of related diseases including Ankylosing Spondylitis (AS), Rheumatoid Arthritis (RA), Osteoarthritis (OA), Juvenile

Idiopathic Arthritis (JIA), fibromyalgia, and gout/hyperuricemia.

Extensive research has revealed that curcumin inhibits the activity of cyclooxygenase-2 (COX-2) and 5-lipoxygenase (5-LOX) enzymes. COX-2 is an enzyme that increases the conversion of arachidonic acid to prostaglandin, which is known to cause inflammation, pain, and blood clotting. 5-lipoxygenase (5-LOX) is an enzyme that accelerates the conversion of arachidonic acid to leukotrienes. Leukotrienes play a critical role in inflammation and allergic reactions. Curcumin stops the conversion of COX-2 and 5-LOX into inflammatory compounds. Curcumin also quenches free radicals in the affected tissues and supports the body's quest toward a healthy, inflammation-free homeostasis (Rao 2007).

Osteoarthritis (OA) is a degenerative joint disease that affects over 40 million Americans and is a leading cause of disability (Ameyde 2022). After reviewing 15 clinical trials, scientists concluded that curcumin supplementation alone can be expected to achieve considerable analgesic effects for patients with symptomatic knee osteoarthritis in the short term without any increase of adverse events (Feng 2022). It relieves pain, improves joint mobility and stiffness, and shortens medication usage in OA patients (Bideshki 2024). In other clinical trials, patients suffering from other types of arthritis reported decreased joint inflammation, less morning stiffness, more walking time, and decreased joint swelling (Pourhabbi-Zarandi 2021). Patients also saw high levels of erythrocyte sedimentation rate (ESR) and C-reactive protein (CRP) return to healthy, normal levels (Kou 2023, Hsueh 2025). Curcumin has similar effects to non-steroidal anti-inflammatory drugs (NSAIDs). However, it has fewer adverse events than these drugs (Wang 2021). To benefit fully from turmeric/curcumin, researchers routinely recommend taking them for a duration of at least 12 weeks for joint pain and/or other inflammation. Additionally, as they recognize the synergistic effects of curcumin and its lack of side effects, enlightened medical doctors recommend the use of curcumin at the same time as anti-inflammatory drugs (Ferguson 2021, Zeng 2022, Wang 2025).

Neurodegenerative Diseases

As human beings age, they become increasingly susceptible to neurodegenerative diseases such as Parkinson's disease, Alzheimer's disease, Huntington's disease, multiple sclerosis, and amyotrophic lateral sclerosis. These conditions cause nerve cell disruption and, in due course, lead to brain cell death (Genchi 2024). Numerous studies have confirmed that curcumin helps prevent or slow down cognitive decline (Reddy 2018).

It is hypothesized that curcumin crosses the blood brain barrier (BBB), reaches brain cells, and protects the neurons from various toxic substances including amyloid-β and tau proteins. Recent research on amyloid-β shows that curcumin prevents this protein fragment from aggregating, thus preventing it from forming plaque, specifically in the regions associated with memory and cognitive functions (Baum 2008, Reddy 2018). Curcumin is also being studied for its possible effects on other neurological diseases such as prions disease, stroke, Down's syndrome, autism, anxiety, depression, and aging (Bhat 2019). Scientists suggest that curcumin shows more of a preventive role than curative one when it comes to alleviating cognitive decline in human populations (Sivanantharajah 2022). Moreover, adding curcumin to traditional drug therapy appears promising and safe for treating neurodegenerative diseases (Bassoli 2023).

In a recent clinical trial, scientists studied the effect of long-term ingestion of curcumin on memory. The subjects were not cognitively impaired, were between the ages of 50 to 90, and took curcumin for 18 months. The researchers observed that curcumin's cognitive benefits include memory improvement and decreased amyloid-β and tau binding in the amygdala and hypothalamus brain areas. This research demonstrated that curcumin has the potential to improve age-related memory decline, prevent or ward off the progression of neurodegeneration, prevent future symptoms of Alzheimer's disease, and improve global cognitive function. The scientists hypothesized that the results stem from curcumin's anti-inflammatory and/or anti-amyloid brain effects. However, to be of value in improving cognitive function, they also pointed out that curcumin should be taken for an extended time-period. They also pointed out that, since it is relatively inexpensive and harmless, curcumin makes an ideal supplement to protect the brain (Small 2018).

Turmeric and curcumin's absorption challenge, or is it?

Turmeric and its curcuminoids are said to be notoriously difficult to absorb into the human digestive system. It is also difficult to detect curcumin in the circulation or target tissues. That has slowed the ability of investigators to prove the herb's direct role on inflamed tissues. However, there is a growing school of thought that suggests that turmeric/curcumin doesn't need to be absorbed to reduce inflammation in the body. Researchers have shown that curcumin decreases the release of gut bacteria-derived lipopolysaccharide (LPS) into the systemic circulation. Curcumin and turmeric improve the integrity of the intestinal barrier function simply by making its way through the digestive tract. The bottom line is that a healthy intestinal function decreases the appearance of metabolic diseases such as diabetes, atherosclerosis, and kidney disease (Ghosh 2018). That's a good thing for human beings.

Some herbalists believe there are ways to make turmeric powder or curcumin easier to assimilate. One solution to increasing the absorption of this herb is to add 3% of trikatu powder to the quantity of turmeric powder to be used. Trikatu is a digestive tonic that makes many difficult-to-absorb nutrients more bioavailable and easier to assimilate. It is made of equal parts of black pepper (*Piper nigrum*), long pepper (*Piper longum*), and ginger (*Zingiber officinale*) powders (Pole 2006). Alan Tillotson (2001), in his book *The One Earth Herbal Sourcebook*, suggests using this mixture of herbs (turmeric and trikatu) for a period of 3 to 4 weeks, followed by a rest period of 1 to 2 weeks. Repeat as necessary. Other herbalists suggest the addition of black pepper, rich in piperine, to turmeric powder or curcumin at the rate of 1% black pepper to 99% turmeric powder. These ingredients are known to increase the absorption of turmeric and curcumin in the gastrointestinal tract (Tillotson 2001, Fan 2013, Francis 2024, Yance 2013).

Conclusion

Daniel Gagnon: "Herbalists suggest the addition of black pepper, rich in piperine, to turmeric powder or curcumin at the rate of 1% black pepper to 99% turmeric powder." *Susan Belsinger*

Over the last 35 years, turmeric and curcumin have been proven to possess excellent antioxidant and anti-inflammatory properties. In most cases, they don't cure diseases. However, they decrease the inflammation that is present in many of these diseases and make them more manageable. They help the body regulate gene expression and inhibit the production of inflammatory mediators. In the treatment of inflammatory bowel disease, arthritis, skin issues, atherosclerosis, cancer, cardiovascular diseases, and many other inflammatory diseases, curcumin and turmeric reduce inflammatory response, effectively improve symptoms, and play a starring part in soothing the tissues (Peng 2021). What makes them an even more obvious choice in so many diseases is that they offer several advantages over drugs, including a high safety profile, low toxicity, easy accessibility, and low cost. They also have a very low herb-to-drug interaction (Fan 2013).

How to Use Turmeric as Medicine

As a mouth wash, especially in mucositis

Dissolve 500 mg (1/4 teaspoon) of turmeric powder in approximately 80 milliliters (about 3 ounces) of boiled and cooled water. Swish the mouth with 10 mL (1/3 of a liquid ounce) of the turmeric solution for about 2 minutes and spit it out. Repeat this procedure 4 times for each swish session. Do this for up to a total of 6 times a day. If receiving radiation, swish 1 hour prior to radiation, 1, 2, 4, and 6 hours after radiation, and once before going to bed. Otherwise, swish every two hours (Rao 2014).

Internally

Turmeric tinctures

Tinctures offer some benefits. Take 30 drops of the liquid herbal extract two to three times a day.

As a turmeric supplement

Take two to eight turmeric rhizome powder capsules (500 mg per capsule) per day ideally in divided doses throughout the day. The higher your inflammation level, the greater the amount of turmeric rhizome powder you can use.

As a curcumin supplement

Take from 500 mg up to 6 grams of curcumin per day. The higher your inflammation level, the greater the amount of curcumin you may use. Dividing it into 4 to 6 dosages during the day is ideal and seems to reduce the inflammation more quickly.

I think that more benefits are derived from the turmeric powder or curcumin as it makes its way through the intestinal tract. There's something that happens between the body and the turmeric constituents as it goes through the digestive system. In term of turmeric in recipes, it's my opinion that any turmeric added to foods is a plus.

Externally

As an eye wash

Turmeric rhizome powder tea is beneficial in soreness of the eyes. Gently boil 2 grams (about one scant teaspoon) of turmeric powder in eight (8) ounces of water till it is reduced to half. Filter and add 1/4 teaspoon of salt to the solution. Let cool to room temperature. A few drops of this herbal tea put in the affected eyes three or four times a day gives significant relief (Bhowmik 2009).

(A solution made from water and salt at the right ratio is called an isotonic solution. When using an isotonic solution, there's no net movement of water into or out of the eye cells, meaning the cells neither shrink nor swell for the water. An isotonic solution mimics tears' salinity and reduces irritation of the eyes.)

Please keep in mind that using turmeric as a tea or a paste will stain the skin around the eye or any other tissues a golden yellow.

Safety

There are no safety concerns surrounding the use of this herb. The Botanical Safety Handbook classifies turmeric as a Safety Class 1 herb, an herb that can be safely consumed when used appropriately (Gardner 2013). No adverse effects from ingestion of turmeric are expected when consumed within the recommended dosage (Bone 2013). As far as curcumin goes, a study by Cheng (2001) demonstrated that curcumin was not toxic to humans when up to 8,000 mg/day was taken orally for 3 months.

Pregnancy and Lactation

The authors of *Botanical Safety Handbook* note that while their review did not identify any concerns for use of turmeric during pregnancy or while nursing, safety has not been conclusively established (Gardner 2013). Contraindications None known (Gardner 2013).

Adverse Effects and Side Effects

Contact dermatitis has been reported in sensitive individuals after topical of turmeric products (Gardner 2013). There's suggestion that high doses of turmeric powder or curcumin may aggravate the gastrointestinal system, that individuals suffering from gastric ulcers or hyperacidity should abstain from taking the product. Conversely, in other individuals, turmeric powder has been shown to heal stomach and intestinal mucous membranes.

Drug Interactions

The Botanical Safety Handbook has classified turmeric as "an herb for which no clinically relevant interactions are expected" (Gardner 2013).

References

Allegri, P., Mastromarino, A., and Neri, P. 2010. "Management of chronic anterior uveitis relapses: Efficacy of oral phospholipidic curcumin treatment. Long-term follow-up." *Clin Ophthamol.* 4: 1201-1206.

Alwi, I., Santoso, T., and Sunyono, S. 2008. "The Effect of Curcumin on Lipid Level in Patients with Acute Coronary Syndrome." *Acta Med Indones-Indones J Intern Med.* 40(4): 201-210.

Ameyde, MV. and Hogden, J. 2022. "In patients with osteoarthritis, is curcumin, compared to placebo, effective in reducing pain?" *J Okla State Med Assoc.* 115(1): 28–30.

Arora, RB., Kapoor, V., Basu, N., Jain, AP. 1971. "Anti-inflammatory studies on *Curcuma longa* (turmeric)." *Indian J Med Res.* 59(8): 1289-1295.

Bartram, T. 1998. *Bartram's Encyclopedia of Herbal Medicine*. London, England: Constable and Robinson Ltd.

Baum, L., Lam, CWK., Cheung, SKK., Kwok, T., Lui, V., Tsoh, J., Lam, L., Leung, V., Hui, E., Ng, C., Woo, J., Chiu, HFK., Goggins, WB., Zee, BCY., Cheng, KF., Fong, CYS., Wong, A., Mok, A., Chow, MSS., Ho, PC., Ip, SP., Ho, CS., Yu, XY., Lai, CYL., Chan, MH., Szeto, S., Chan, HIS., and Mok,

V. 2008. "Six-Month Randomized, Placebo-Controlled, Double-Blind, Pilot Clinical Trial of Curcumin in Patients with Alzheimer Disease." *Journal of Clinical Psychopharmacology*. 28(1): 110-113.

Bhat, A., Mahalakshmi, AM., Ray. B., Tuladhar. S., Hediyal., TA., Manthiannem, E., Padamati, J., Chandra, R., Chidambaram, SB. And Sakharkar, MK. 2019. "Benefits of curcumin in brain disorders." *BioFactors*. 2019;1–24.

Bhowmik, D., Chiranjib, KP., Kumar, S., Chandira, M. and B. Jayakar. 2009. "Turmeric: An Herbal and Traditional Medicine." *Archives of Applied Science Research*. 1(2): 86-108.

Bideshki. MV., Jourabchi-Ghadim N., Radkhah, N., Behzadi, N., Asemani, S., Jamilian, P. and Zarezadeh, M. 2024. "The efficacy of curcumin in relieving osteoarthritis: A meta-analysis of meta-analyses." *Phytother Res*. 38(6): 2875-2891.

Blumenthal, M. editor. 2014. "2013 Herb Market Report." *HerbalGram*. 103: 58-62.

_____, M. editor. 2024. "2023 Herb Market Report." *HerbalGram*. 133: 58-62.

Bone, K. 2003 *A Clinical Guide to Blending Liquid Herbs*. St. Louis, MO: Elsevier Churchill Livingstone.

Bone. K. and Mills, S. 2013. *Principles and Practice of Phytotherapy*. 2nd edition. London, England: Churchill Livingstone.

Bruneton, J. 1987. *Éléments de Phytochimie et de Pharmacognosie*. Paris, France. Lavoisider.

Buonomo, AR., Scotto, R., Nappa, S., Arcopinto, M., Salzano, A., Marra, AM., D'Assante, R., Zappulo, E., Borgia, G. and Gentile, I. 2019. "The role of curcumin in liver diseases." *Arch Med Sci. 6*: 1608-1620.

Caldecott, T. 2006 *Ayurveda: The Divine Science of Life*. Philadelphia, PA: Mosby Elsevier.

Castleman, M. 1991. *The Healing Herbs*. Emmaus, PA: Rodale Press.

Chandrasekaran, PR., Madanagopalan, VG. 2022. . "Role of Curcumin in Retinal Diseases-A review." *Graefe's Archive for Clinical and Experimental Ophthalmology*. 260: 1457–1473.

Chattopadhyayl, I., Biwas, K., Bondyopadhyay, U. and Banerjee, R.K. 2004. "Turmeric and curcumin: Biological actions and medicinal applications." *Current Science*. 87(1): 44-53.

Chen J, and T. Chen. 2001. *Chinese Medical Herbology and Pharmacology*.

City of Industry, CA: Art of Medicine Press, Inc.

Chen, M., Hu, DN., Pan, Z., Lu, CW., Xue, CY. and Aass, I. 2010. "Curcumin protects against hyperosmoticity-induced IL-1b elevation in human corneal epithelial cell via MAPK pathways." *Experimental Eye Research* 90: 437-443.

Cheng, AL., Hsu, CH., Lin, JK., Hsu, MM., Ho, YF., Shen, TS., Ko, JY., Lin, JT., Lin, BR., Ming-Shiang, W., Yu, HS., Jee, SH., Chen, GS., Chen, TM., Chen, CA., Lai, MK., Pu, YS., Pan, MH., Wang, YJ., Tsai, CC., and CY Hsieh. 2001. "Phase I clinical trial of curcumin, a chemopreventive agent, in patients with high-risk or pre-malignant lesions." *Anticancer Res.* 21(4B): 2895-900.

Chin, WY., and Keng, H. 1992. *An Illustrated Dictionary of Chinese Medicinal Herbs*. Sebastopol, CA: CRCS Publications.

Chitra, R. 2016. "Effect of Planting Material on Growth and Yield of Turmeric." *Madras Agric. J.* 103 (10-12): 366-369.

Christopher, J. 1976. *School of Natural Healing*. Provo, UT: BiWorld Publishers, Inc.

Coelho, MR., Romi, MD., Ferreira, DMTP., Zaltman, C. and Soares-Mota, M. 2020. "The Use of Curcumin as a Complementary Therapy in Ulcerative Colitis: A Systematic Review of Randomized Controlled Clinical Trials." *Nutrients*. 12(2296): 1-12.

Cozmin, M., Lungu, II., Gutu, C., Stefanache, A., Duceac, LD., Soltuzu, BD, Calin, G., Bogdan, ER., Grierosu, C., Boev. 2024. "Turmeric: from spice to cure. A review of the anti-cancer, radioprotective and anti-inflammatory effects of turmeric sourced compounds." *Front. Nutr.* 11: 1-12.

Cox, F.F., Misiou, A., Vierkant, A., Ale-Agha, N., Grandoch, M., Haendeler, J., Altschmied, J. 2022. "Protective Effects of Curcumin in Cardiovascular Diseases—Impact on Oxidative Stress and Mitochondria." *Cells.* 11 (342): 1-24.

Dahka, SM., Afsharfar, M., Tajadod, S., Sohouli, MH., Shekari. S., Nafouti, FB., Alizadeh, A., Kachaei, HS., Abbasi, K., Mohseni, JK., Alami, F., Gholamalizadeh1, M. and Doaei1. S. 2025. "Impact of Curcumin Supplementation on Radiation Dermatitis Severity: A Systematic Review and Meta-Analysis of Randomized Controlled Trials." *Asian Pacific Journal of Cancer Prevention.* 24: 783-789.

Duke, J. 1985. *Handbook of Medicinal Herbs*. Boca Raton, FL: CRC Press.

___. 2002. *Handbook of Medicinal Herbs*. Boca Raton, FL: CRC Press.

Evans, W. 1989. *Trease and Evans' Pharmacognosy*. 13th edition. London, England: Bailliere Tindall.

Evans, W. 1996. *Trease and Evans' Pharmacognosy*. 14th edition. London, England: WB Saunders Co. Ltd.

Fan, X., Zhang, C., Liu, D., Yan, J., and Liang, H. 2013. "The Clinical Applications of Curcumin: Current State and the Future." Current Pharmaceutical Design. 19(11): 2011–2031.

Feng, J., Li, Z., Tian, L., Mu, P., Hu, Y., Xiong, F. and Ma, X. 2022. "Efficacy and safety of curcuminoids alone in alleviating pain and dysfunction for knee osteoarthritis: a systematic review and meta-analysis of randomized controlled trials." *BMC: Complementary Medicine and Therapies*. 22: 276-297.

Ferguson, JJA., Kylie, JA., Abbott, A., and Manohar, L. 2021. "Anti-inflammatory effects of oral supplementation with curcumin: a systematic review and meta-analysis of randomized controlled trials." *Nutrition Reviews*, 79 (9): 1043–1066,

Francis, AJ., Sreenivasan, C., Parikh, A., et al. 2024. "Curcumin and Cognitive Function: A Systematic Review of the Effects of Curcumin on Adults with and without Neurocognitive Disorders." *Cureus.* 16(8): 1-12.

Franzone, F., Nebbioso, M., Pergolizzi, T., Attanasio, G., Musacchio, A., Greco, A., Limoli, PG., Artico, M., Spandidos, DA., Taurone, S., and Agostinelli S. 2021. "Anti-inflammatory role of curcumin in retinal disorders (Review)." *Experimental and Therapeutic Medicine*. 22(790): 1-7.

Frawley, D. 2000. *Ayurvedic Healing*. Twin Lakes, WI: Lotus Press.

Frawley, D. and V. Lad. 2001. *The Yoga of Herbs*. 2nd edition. Twin Lakes, WI: Lotus Press.

Ganesan, R. 2015. "Growth and instability in area, production and productivity of turmeric in selected states in India." *Journal of Management and Science*. 5(4): 301-311.

Gardner, Z. and McGuffin, M. editors. 2013. *Botanical Safety Handbook,* 2 ed. Boca Raton, FL: CRC Press.

Genchi, G., Lauria, G., Catalano, A.. Carocci, A., and Sinicropi, MS. 2024. "Neuroprotective Effects of Curcumin in Neurodegenerative Diseases." *Foods.* 13 (1774): 1-24.

Ghosh, SS., He, H., Wang, J., Gehr, TW. and Ghosh, S. 2018. "Curcumin-mediated regulation of intestinal barrier function: The mechanism underlying its beneficial effects." *Tissue Barriers*. 6(1): 1-13.

Gogte, VM. 2017. *Ayurvedic Pharmacology and Therapeutic Uses of Medicinal Plants*. New Delhi, India. Chaukhambha Publications.

Granger, DN., and Senchenkova, E. 2010. "Inflammation and the Microcirculation." San Raphael, CA: *Morgan and Claypool Life Sciences*.

Grieve, M. 1982. *A Modern Herbal*. NY, NY: Dover Publications, Inc. (reprint of 1931 ed.).

Guenther, E. 1952. *The Essential Oils*. Volume V. Malabar, FL: Robert E. Krieger Publishing Co., Inc.

Goulart, RdA., Barbalho, SM., Lima, VM., de Souza, GA., Julia Novaes Matias, JN., Arau´jo, AC., Rubira, CJ., Buchaim, RL. Buchaim, DV., de Carvalho, ACA and Guiguer, EL. 2020. "Effects of the Use of Curcumin on Ulcerative Colitis and Crohn's Disease: A Systematic Review. " *J Med Food*. 1–11.

Hay, E., Lucariello, A., Contieria, M., Esposito, T., De Luca, A., Guerra, G. and Pernad, A. 2019. "Therapeutic effects of turmeric in several diseases: An overview." 2019. *Chemico-Biological Interactions*. 1-6.

He, Y., Yue, Y., Zheng, X., Zhang, K., Chen, S., and Du, Z. 2015. "Curcumin, Inflammation, and Chronic Diseases: How Are They Linked?" *Molecules*. 20(5): 9183–9213.

Hegde, M., Girisa, S., BharathwajChetty, B., Vishwa, R. and Kunnumakkara, AB. 2023. "Curcumin Formulations for Better Bioavailability: What We Learned from Clinical Trials Thus Far?" *ACS Omega*. 8: 10713–10746.

Hengge, UH., Ruzicka, T., Schwartz. RA., and Cork. MJ. 2006. "Adverse effects of topical glucocorticosteroids." *J Am Acad Dermatol*. 54 (1): 1-15.

Hoffmann, D. 1983. *The New Holistic Herbal*. Rockport, MA: Element Books Limited.

Hsueh, HC., Ho, JR., Tzeng, SI., Liang HI. and Horng, YS. 2025. "Effects of curcumin on serum inflammatory biomarkers in patients with knee osteoarthritis: a systematic review and meta-analysis of randomized controlled trials." *BMC Complementary Medicine and Therapies*. 25:237: 1-17.

Hussain, Y., Alam, W., Ullah, H., Dacrema, M., Daglia, M., Khan, H., and Arciola, CR. 2022. "Antimicrobial Potential of Curcumin: Therapeutic Potential and Challenges to Clinical Applications." *Antibiotics* 11: 322-354.

Indriyani, N. and Nur'aeny, N. 2025. "The Therapeutic Effects of Curcumin on Oral Disease: A Systematic Review." *Clinical Pharmacology: Advances and Applications*. 17: 13-24.

Jadhav, VG., Bahviskar, PP., Waghmare, SN., and Bhosale, SN. 2022. "Export performance of Turmeric in India." *The Pharma Innovation Journal.* SP-11(1): 425-427.

Jager PD. 1997. *Turmeric.* California: Vidyasagar Pub; p. 67.

Jäger, R., Lowery, RP., Calvanese, AV., Joy, JM., Purpura, M. and Wilson, JW. 2014. "Comparative absorption of curcumin formulations." *Nutrition Journal.* 13 (11): 1-8.

Jiang, T., Ghosh, R., and Charcosset, C. 2021. "Extraction, purification and applications of curcumin from plant materials - A comprehensive review." *Trends in Science and Technology.* 112: 419-430.

Jyotirmayee, B., and Mahalik, G. 2022. "Traditional Uses and Variation in Curcumin Content in Varieties of Curcuma - the Saffron of India." *Ambient Science.* 09(1): 6-12.

Kapoor, LD. 2001. *Handbook of Ayurvedic Medicinal Plants.* Boca Raton, FL: CRC Press.

Kasprzak-Drozd, K., Nizinski, P., Hawry, A., Gancarz, M., Hawrył, D., Oliwa, W., Pałka, M., Markowska, J. and Oniszczuk, A. 2024. "Potential of Curcumin in the Management of Skin Diseases." Int. J. Mol. Sci. 25 (3617): 1-17.

Kloss, J. 1975. *Back to Eden.* Santa Barbara, CA: Woodbridge Press Publishing Company.

Kong, WY., Ngai, SC., Goh, BH., Lee, LH., Htar, T.T., and Chuah, LH. 2021. "Is Curcumin the Answer to Future Chemotherapy Cocktail?" *Molecules.* 26, 4329 1-47.

Kou, H., Huang, L., Jin, M., He, Q., Zhang, R. and Ma, J. 2023. "Effect of curcumin on rheumatoid arthritis: a systematic review and meta-analysis." *Front. Immunol.* 14: 1-11.

Kuhn, M. and D. Winston. 2001 *Herbal Therapy and Supplements.* Philadelphia, PA: Lippincott Williams and Wilkins.

Kumar, A., Harsha, C., Parama, D., Girisa, S., Daimary, U. D., Mao, X., and Kunnumakkara, A. B. 2021. "Current clinical developments in curcumin□ based therapeutics for cancer and chronic diseases." *Phytotherapy Research.* 1-34.

Kunnumakkara, AB., Anand, P. and Aggarwal, BB. 2008. "Curcumin inhibits proliferation, invasion, angiogenesis and metastasis of different cancers through interaction with multiple cell signaling proteins." *Cancer Letters.* 269: 199–225.

Kunnumakkara, AB., Bordoloi, D., Padmavathi, G., Monisha, J., Roy, NK., Prasad, S. and Aggarwal, BB. 2017. "Curcumin, the golden nutraceutical: multitargeting for multiple chronic diseases." *British Journal of Pharmacology*. 174: 1325–1348.

Kunnumakkara, AB., Hegde, M., Parama, D., Girisa, S., Kumar, A., Daimary, UD., Garodia, P., Yenisetti, SC., Oommen, OV., and Bharat B. Aggarwal, BB. 2023. "Role of Turmeric and Curcumin in Prevention and Treatment of Chronic Diseases: Lessons Learned from Clinical Trials." *ACS Pharmacol. Transl. Sci.* 6: 447−518.

Lal, B., Kapoor, AK., Asthana, OP., Agrawal, PK., Prasad, R., Kumar, P. and Srimal, RC. 1999. "Efficacy of Curcumin in the Management of Chronic Anterior Uveitis." *Phytother Research.* 13: 318–322.

Leclerc, H. 1929. *Les Épices*. Paris, France: Masson.

Lee, YM., and Kim, Y. 2024. "Is Curcumin Intake Really Effective for Chronic Inflammatory Metabolic Disease? A Review of Meta-Analyses of Randomized Controlled Trials." *Nutrients.* 16, 1728.

Leonard, DB. 2025. website: https://www.herbrally.com/monograph/turmeric Accessed on July 7, 2025.

Leung, A. and S. Foster. 1996. *Encyclopedia of Common Natural Ingredients used in Food, Drugs and Cosmetics.* 2nd edition. New York, NY: John Wiley & Sons, Inc.

Li, T., Jin, J., Pu, F., Bai, Y., Chen, Y., Li, Y. and Wang, X. 2023. "Cardioprotective effects of curcumin against myocardial I/R injury: A systematic review and meta-analysis of preclinical and clinical studies." *Front. Pharmacol.* 14(1111459): 1-26.

Liu, XF., Hao, JL., Xie, T., Mukhtar, NJ., Zhang, W., Malik, TH., Lu, CW. and Zhou, DD. 2017. "Curcumin, A Potential Therapeutic Candidate for Anterior Segment Eye Diseases: A Review." *Front. Pharmacol.* 8 (66): 1-13.

Lopez-Lazaro, M. 2008. "Anticancer and carcinogenic properties of curcumin: Considerations for its clinical development as a cancer chemopreventive and chemotherapeutic agent." *Mol. Nutr. Food Res*. 52: S103 – S127.

Lopresti, AL., Smith, SJ., Rea, A. and Michel, S. 2021. "Efficacy of a curcumin extract (Curcugen™) on gastrointestinal symptoms and intestinal microbiota in adults with self-reported digestive complaints: a randomised, double-blind, placebo-controlled study." *BMC Complementary Medicine and Therapies.* 21 (40): 1-17.

Lust, J. 1974. *The Herb Book.* Simi Valley, CA: Benedict Lust Publications.

Mallo, N., Lamas, J., Sueiro, RA. and Leiro, JM. 2020. "Molecular Targets Implicated in the Antiparasitic and Anti-Inflammatory Activity of the Phytochemical Curcumin in Trichomoniasis." *Molecules.* 25: 1-14.

Mansouri, K., Rasoulpoor, S., Daneshkhah, A., Abolfathi, S., Salari, N., Mohammadi, M., Rasoulpoor, S., and Shabani. S. 2020. "Clinical effects of curcumin in enhancing cancer therapy: A systematic review." *BMC Cancer.* 20 (1): 791, 1-11.

Mata, IR. da, Mata, SR. da, Menezes, RCR., Faccioli, LS., Bandeira, KK., and Bosco, SMD. 2020. "Benefits of turmeric supplementation for skin health in chronic diseases: a systematic review." *Critical Reviews in Food Science and Nutrition.* 1–15.

McCormick & Co. 1979. *Spices of the World Cookbook by McCormick.* Revised Edition. New York, NY.: McGraw Hill Book Company.

Menzies-Trull, C. 2003. *Herbal Medicine, Keys to Physiomedicalism including Pharmacopoeia.* Newcastle, England: Faculty of Physiomedical Herbal Medicine.

Mills, S. 1991. *Out of the Earth.* New York, NY: Viking Arcana.

Mohammadi, SG., Kafeshani, M., Bagherniya, M., Kesharwani, P., and Sahebkar, A. 2024. "Exploring Curcumin's healing properties in the treatment of atopic dermatitis." *Food Bioscience.* 59:

Mortezaee, K., Salehi, E., Mirtavoos-mahyari, H., Motevaseli, E., Najafi, M., Farhood, B., Rosengren, R., Sahebkar, A. 2019. "Mechanisms of apoptosis modulation by curcumin: Implications for cancer therapy." *J Cell Physiol.* 1-14.

Mohseni, S., Tavakoli, A., Ghazipoor, H., Pouralimohamadi, N., Zare, R., Rampp, T., Shayesteh, M. and Pasalar, M. 2025. "Curcumin for the clinical treatment of inflammatory bowel diseases: a systematic review and meta-analysis of placebo-controlled randomized clinical trials." *Front. Nutr.* 12:1494351.

Nabhan, GP. 2014. *Cumin, Camels, and Caravans: A Spice Odyssey.* Berkeley, CA: University of California Press.

Nagpal, M, and Sood, S. 2013. "Role of curcumin in systemic and oral health: An overview." *Journal of Natural Science, Biology and Medicine.* 4(1): 3-7.

Ng, QX., Soh, AYS., Loke, W., Venkatanarayanan, N., Lim, DW. and Yeo

WS. 2018. "A Meta-Analysis of the Clinical Use of Curcumin for Irritable Bowel Syndrome (IBS)." *J. Clin. Med.* 7 (298): 1-9.

Pakfetrat, M., Basiri, F., Malekmakan, L., and Roozbeh, J. 2014. "Effects of turmeric on uremic pruritus in end stage renal disease patients: a double-blind randomized clinical trial." *Journal of Nephrology.* 27(2): 203–207.

Panknin, TM., Howe, CL., Hauer, M., Bucchireddigari, B., Rossi, AM.; and Funk, JL. 2023. "Curcumin Supplementation and Human Disease: A Scoping Review of Clinical Trials." *Int. J. Mol. Sci.* 24 4476: 1-22.

Peng, Y., Ao, M., Dong, B., Jiang, Y., Yu, L., Chen, Z., Hu, C. and Xu, R. 2021. "Anti-Inflammatory Effects of Curcumin in the Inflammatory Diseases: Status, Limitations and Countermeasures." *Drug Design, Development and Therapy.* 15: 4503-4525.

Peng, Y. Li, D., Wu, N., Wang, XY., Sun, GX., Gao, HB. and Li, HX. 2025. "Safety and efficacy of curcumin in the treatment of ulcerative colitis: an updated systematic review and meta-analysis of randomized controlled trials." *Explore* 21: 103803: 1-9.

Pengelly, A. 2004. *The Constituents of Medicinal Plants.* 2nd edition. Cambridge, MA; CABI Publishing,

Pescosolido, N., Giannotti, R., Plateroti, A., Pascarella, A. and Nebbioso, M. 2013. "Curcumin: Therapeutical Potential in Ophthalmology." *Planta Medica.* 80(04): 249–254.

Pole, S. 2006. *Ayurvedic Medicine: The Principles of Traditional Practice.* Philadelphia, PA: Churchill Livingstone Elsevier.

Pourhabibi-Zarandi1, F., Shojaei-Zarghani, S. and Rafraf, M. 2021. "Curcumin and rheumatoid arthritis: A systematic review of literature. " *International Journal of Clinical Practice.*

Prasad S. and Aggarwal, BB. 2011. "Turmeric, the Golden Spice. From Traditional Medicine to Modern Medicine." In I. F. F. Benzie, S. Wachtel-Galor S. (eds). 2011 *Herbal Medicine: Biomolecular and Clinical Aspects. 2nd edition.* Boca Raton, FL: CRC Press/Taylor & Francis, 263-288.

Prasad, S., Gupta, S. C., Tyagi, AK., and Aggarwal, BB. 2014. "Curcumin, a component of golden spice: From bedside to bench and back." *Biotechnology Advances.* 32(6): 1053–1064.

Prucksunand, CH., Kiatying-Aiigsulee, N., Sawasdimongkol, K., Wimolwattanapun, S., Petchruengrong, B., Tiensong, K. and S. Paeyai1. 1997. "Prevention Action of Turmeric against HCl-induced Gastric Necrosis in Rat: to Verify the Mode of Action of Previous Clinical Study." *Thai J. Pharm. Sci..*21(1): 43-48.

Radomska-Leśniewska, DM., Osiecka-Iwan, A., Hyc, A., Góźdź, A., Dąbrowska, AM., and Skopiński, P. 2019. "Therapeutic potential of curcumin in eye diseases." *Central European Journal of Immunology.* 44(2): 181–189.

Rao, CV. 2007. "Regulation of COX and LOX by curcumin." *Advances in experimental medicine and biology. Found in The Molecular Targets and Therapeutic Uses of Curcumin in Health and Diseases.* Vol 595.

Rao, S., Dinkar, C., Vaishnav, LK., Rao, P., Rai, MP., Fayad, R., and Baliga, MS. 2014. "The Indian Spice Turmeric Delays and Mitigates Radiation-Induced Oral Mucositis in Patients Undergoing Treatment for Head and Neck Cancer: An Investigational Study." *Integr Cancer Ther.* 13: 201-212.

Ravindran, PN., Babu, KN., and Sivaraman, K. 2007. *Turmeric The Genus Curcuma.* Boca Raton, FL: CRC Press (Taylor & Francis Group).

Reddy, PH., Manczak, M., Yin, X., Grady1, MC., Mitchell, A., Tonk, S., Kuruva, CS., Bhatti, JS., Kandimalla1, R., Vijayan, M., Kumar, S., Wang, R., Pradeepkiran, JA., Ogunmokun, G., Thamarai, K., Quesada, K., Boles, A., and Reddy, AP. 2018. "Protective Effects of Indian Spice Curcumin Against Amyloid Beta in Alzheimer's Disease." *J Alzheimers Dis.* 61(3): 843–866.

Schaffner, W. 1993. *Les plantes médicinales et leur propriétés.* Lausanne, Switzerland : Delachaux et Niestlé.

Sidhu, GS., Mani, H., Gaddipati, JP., Singh, AK., Seth, P., Banaudha, KK., Patnaik, GK., and Maheshwari, RK. 1999. "Curcumin enhances wound healing in streptozotocin induced diabetic rats and genetically diabetic mice." *Wound Repair and Regeneration.* 7(5): 362–374.

Sivanantharajah L and Mudher A. 2022. "Curcumin as a Holistic Treatment for Tau Pathology*." Front. Pharmacol.* 13:903119.

Skenderi, G. 2003. *Herbal Vade Mecum.* Rutherford, NJ: Herbacy Press.

Small, G. W., Siddarth, P., Li, Z., Miller, KJ., Ercoli, L., Emerson, ND., Martinez, J., Wong, KP., Liu, J., Merrill, DA., Chen, ST., Henning, SM., Satyamurthy, N., Huang, SC., Heber, D., and Barrio, JR. 2018. "Memory and Brain Amyloid and Tau Effects of a Bioavailable Form of Curcumin in Non-Demented Adults: A Double-Blind, Placebo-Controlled 18-Month Trial." *The American Journal of Geriatric Psychiatry.* 26(3): 266–277.

Srimal, RC., Khanna, NM., and Dhawan, BN. 1971. *"*A preliminary report on anti-inflammatory activity of curcumin." *Indian Journal of Pharmacology.* 3:10.

Srimal, RC., and Dhawan, BN. 1973. "Pharmacology of diferuloyl methane (curcumin), a non-steroidal anti-inflammatory agent." *J. Pharm. Pharmac.* 25: 447-452.

Teuscher, E., Anton, R., and Lobstein. A. 2005. *Plantes aromatiques.* Paris, France: Éditions Tec et Doc.

Tillotson, AK. 2001. *The One Earth Herbal Sourcebook.* New York, NY: Kensington Books.

"Turmeric Outlook.", March 2025 Professor Jayashankar Telangana Agricultural University. https://www.pjtau.edu.in › files › AgriMkt › Turm. Accessed 6/10/2025.

Tyler, V. 1993. *The Honest Herbal.* 3rd edition. Binghampton, NY: The Haworth Press.

Uphof, J.C. 1968. *Dictionary of Economic Plants.* New York, NY. Stechert-Harner Service Agency, Inc.

Valnet, J. 1992. *Phytothérapie.* Paris, France: Maloine.

Van Hellemont, J. 1986. *Compendium de Phytothérapie.* Brussels, Belgium: Association Pharmaceutique Belge.

Vanaie, A., Shahidi, S., Iraj, B., Siadat, ZD., Kabirzade, M., Shakiba, F., Mohammadi, M., and H. Parvizian. 2019. "Curcumin as a major active component of turmeric attenuates proteinuria in patients with overt diabetic nephropathy." *J Res Med Sci.* 24(77).

Vaughn, AR., Branum, A., and Sivamani, RK. 2016. "Effects of Turmeric (*Curcuma longa*) on Skin Health: A Systematic Review of the Clinical Evidence." *Phytotherapy Research.* 30(8): 1243–1264.

Vera-Ramirez, L., Pérez-Lopez, P., Varela-Lopez, A., Ramirez-Tortosa, Mc., Battino, M., and Quiles, JL. 2013. "Curcumin and liver disease." *BioFactors.* 39(1): 88–100.

Wang, Z., Singh, A., Jones, G., Winzenberg, T., Ding, C., Chopra, A., Das, S., Danda, D., Laslett, L. and Antony, B. 2021. "Efficacy and Safety of Turmeric Extracts for the Treatment of Knee Osteoarthritis: A Systematic Review and Meta-analysis of Randomised Controlled Trials." *Current Rheumatology Reports.* 23(2): 1-9.

Wang, W., Zhao, R., Liu, B., and Li, K. 2025. "The effect of curcumin supplementation on cognitive function: an updated systematic review and meta-analysis." *Front. Nutr.* 12:1549509.

Weiss, R. 1988. *Herbal Medicine.* Beaconsfield, England: Beaconsfield Publishers Ltd.

Wichtl, M. (Ed.) 2004. *Herbal Drugs and Phytopharmaceuticals.* 3 ed.

Boca Raton, FL: CRC Press.

Wilken, R., Veena, MS., Wang, MB., and Srivatsan, ES. 2011. "Curcumin: A review of anti-cancer properties and therapeutic activity in head and neck squamous cell carcinoma." *Molecular Cancer*. 10(1): 12-31.

Williamson, E., editor. (2002) *Major Herbs of Ayurveda*. London, England: Churchill Livingstone.

Wongcharoen, W., and Phrommintikul, A. 2009. "The protective role of curcumin in cardiovascular diseases." *International Journal of Cardiology*. 133(2): 145–151.

Wongcharoen, W., Jai-aue, S., Phrommintikul, A., Nawarawong, W., Woragidpoonpol, S., Tepsuwan, T., Sukonthasarn, A., Apaijai, N., and Chattipakorn, N. 2012. "Effects of Curcuminoids on Frequency of Acute Myocardial Infarction After Coronary Artery Bypass Grafting." *The American Journal of Cardiology*. 110(1): 40–44.

Wren, RB. 1988. Potter's New Cyclopaedia of Botanical Drugs and Preparations. Revised by E. Williamson. Essex, England: The C.W. Daniel Company Limited.

Wronski, P.; Wronski, S.; Kurant, M.; Malinowski, B.; Wicinski, M. 2022. "Curcumin May Prevent Basement Membrane Disassembly by Matrix Metalloproteinases and Progression of the Bladder Cancer." Nutrients. 14(32): 1-22.

Yance, D. 2013. *Adaptogens in Medical Herbalism*. Rochester, VT: Healing Arts Press.

Yen, KY. 1992. *The Illustrated Chinese Materia Medica*. Taipei, Taiwan: SMC Publishing Inc.

Zeng, L., Yang, T., Yang, K., Yu, G., Li, J., Xiang, W. and Chen, H. 2022. "Efficacy and Safety of Curcumin and Curcuma longa Extract in the Treatment of Arthritis: A Systematic Review and Meta-Analysis of Randomized Controlled Trial." *Front. Immunol.* 13:891822.

Zhang, S., Wang, J., Liu, L., Sun, X., Zhou, Y., Chen, S., Lu, Y., Cai, X., Hu, M., Yan, G., Miao, X. and Li X. 2022. "Efficacy and safety of curcumin in psoriasis: preclinical and clinical evidence and possible mechanisms." *Front. Pharmacol.* 13: 1-14.

Zimmermann, M., Johnson, H., McGuffin, M. and Applequist, W. 2023. AHPA's *Herbs of Commerce*, 3rd Edition. Silver Spring, MD: American Herbal Products Association.

Daniel Gagnon, Medical Herbalist, MS, RH (AHG) is a French-Canadian originally from Northern Ontario who relocated to Santa Fe, NM in 1979. He has been a Medical Herbalist since 1976. For over 45 years he worked in the herbal medicine manufacturing sector and was the owner of Herbs, Etc., Inc. manufacturing as well as the retail store located in Santa Fe, NM. As of 2025, he has sold the manufacturing and mail order entity and closed the retail store. Daniel is the author of *The Practical Guide to Herbal Medicines*, a book designed to provide herbal health care options. With Amadea Morningstar, he is also the co-author of *Breathe Free*, a book on healing the respiratory system. He regularly teaches herbal therapeutics both nationally and internationally. Daniel can be reached at botandan@aol.com.

Fall harvest of homegrown turmeric rhizomes from Helen's Fat Cat Farm. *Helen Lowe Metzman*

Ingredients for making a turmeric tincture with either fresh or dried rhizomes. *Susan Belsinger*

Making Turmeric a Part of Our Everyday Life

Carol Little

Don't quote me, but I've heard it said, over the years, that turmeric is the most studied herb on the planet. That's quite the claim to fame! The ongoing turmeric research is simply too astounding to ignore.

Generally it is believed that turmeric may help to prevent or treat: acne, allergies, Alzheimer's disease, arthritis—both osteo and rheumatoid, asthma, cancer, cholesterol, colitis, cystic fibrosis, depression, diabetes (Type 2), digestive disorders, eczema, flatulence, gout, gum disease, heart disease, hypertension, liver disease, macular degeneration (age related), Parkinson's Disease, psoriasis, scleroderma, stroke, and wounds.

People around the world are using turmeric in so many ways. These ideas are from my own life— how I use turmeric in my herbal practice and in my own personal "everyday." I hope you'll be inspired to embrace this golden treasure from our beloved green world.

I always suggest purchasing the fresh root in small quantities and using it quickly. Replace turmeric powder every 6 months. In my herbal practice I love to teach clients, family and friends about easy ways to use good quality turmeric root powder to make concoctions that we can use often to support ourselves. The best quality turmeric powder is freshly ground from the dried rhizomes; however, it can be quite hard to grind.

The general rule of thumb for converting dried herbs or spices to fresh in a recipe is 1 to 3, so 1 teaspoon of dried spice is equal to 3 teaspoons fresh (3 teaspoons = 1 tablespoon). Roughly 2 inches of fresh turmeric root will yield 1 tablespoon of freshly grated root.

Turmeric has a warm, peppery, slightly bitter flavour and a mild fragrance which reminds me of a gingery, orange mix. It can be harsh when eaten raw, so always add it to your cooking or make sure it is slightly heated to enjoy the delicate flavour.

We can all benefit from reducing inflammation in our bodies. Oxidation has been called a kind of internal rust which is caused by molecules which are missing an electron from their outer shell. This process of a molecule stealing an electron from other molecules creates oxidative stress or oxidative damage and results in chronic low-grade inflammation, which in turn has been proven to trigger many diseases.

Turmeric's strength as an antioxidant has been noticed by the world's mainstream medicine and many studies are now singing the praises of its effectiveness. Possibly the most interest in curcumin revolves around the ability to fight cancer on so many levels.

Turmeric Tincture (Folk Method)

This is how I use fresh turmeric root to make an effective tincture. The exact amounts will vary based on the size of the jar or the amount of plant material on hand.

Chop the turmeric root into small pieces, approximately 1/4 inch long, or smaller. This may depend on the size of your turmeric roots. I suggest using a cutting board that is fine to be stained yellow!

Add the roots to a clean glass jar. Ideally, I like to fill the jar to about an inch from the top. Add the alcohol you are using. Typically, people use 100 proof vodka to make a simple but effective tincture. Fill the jar to the top, covering all the plant material. Add a good fitting lid. Label the jar with the herb info/date/type of alcohol used.

Keep the jar nearby and out of direct sunlight so that you can infuse your energy into the medicine with a good few shakes every day or so. Some say tinctures are ready after 2 to 3 weeks, but I prefer to allow to steep for a minimum of 1 month. Many of my tinctures sit for a few months.

To strain, assemble a large funnel, some unbleached cheesecloth, and a clean amber glass bottle.

Place the cheesecloth in the funnel and place into the mouth of the glass bottle. Slowly pour the infused alcohol into the funnel. Scrunch up the cheesecloth around the turmeric roots; squeeze tightly to coax out as much of the alcohol as possible. Compost the roots. Label the amber glass bottle with the herb info/straining date/type of alcohol used.

Recommended Dose

A typical dosage is 1 to 2 mL (which is about 20 to 40 drops) 3 times daily. I always suggest that people start with a loading dose or 1 dropperful to start, 3 times daily. After a few days, if no discomfort is noted, increase the dose to 2 dropperfuls and then up to the 'therapeutic' dose of 3 dropperfuls, 3 times, with some food each day.

Generally, when we take herbs as a part of a daily tonic protocol, we would typically take 'away from food' and the exact recommendations will depend on the individual situation. It's thought that these tinctures taken alone help to increase the body's absorption ability.

Turmeric, however, has its own rhythm for best use because of how curcumin works in the body.

If we are using turmeric as a daily tonic and/or for general inflammation support, it's best to take with meals, especially with breakfast or lunch. Mix into a little water or tea. Curcumin absorbs best with fat and black pepper, so ideally, take it with any food containing oil, nut butter, avocado, etc., and consider adding a pinch of black pepper. Some herbalists also suggest an advantage to adding some ginger tincture for the same reason.

For digestive support, it can be taken 20 minutes prior to meal. However, some folks find it irritating with no food in the mix.

Caution: Consult a health care practitioner prior to using if you are on blood thinners, if you are pregnant, if you have gallstones or a bile duct obstruction, or if you have stomach ulcers or excess stomach acid, or if symptoms persist or worsen.

**bright golden orange
hued earthy flavored rhizome
inflammation aid**

Susan Belsinger

A Journey in Gold

Dorene Petersen

My journey with turmeric began in the bustling spice markets of Morocco and Istanbul and continued through the golden fields of India and Indonesia. With every stop, I learned something new—how this vibrant root colors dishes, anchors rituals, and offers its healing touch across generations.

In Bali and Kerala, southern India, I saw turmeric, *Curcuma longa* L., used in rituals to bless marriages and purify spaces. In Marrakesh and Istanbul, spice sellers built perfect pyramids of turmeric powder, glowing yellow and orange under dusty market light. Their rich, yellow-burnt orange color reflects unique terroirs and curcuminoid content. Turmeric's golden hue signifies health, prosperity, and sacred protection; it is a culinary staple and a living symbol of cultural identity and spiritual continuity.

At ACHS.edu, our students have explored turmeric through study abroad fieldwork and now carefully curated lab kits, discovering how this ancient plant bridges ethnobotany, chemistry, and healing.

Turmeric cones at a Marrakesh spice market in Morocco. In Marrakesh and Istanbul, spice sellers built perfect pyramids of turmeric powder, glowing yellow and orange under dusty market light. *Dorene Petersen*

American College of Healthcare Sciences (ACHS) Silk, Spice, and Sandalwood: An Aromatic Journey Through India study abroad program. *Dorene Petersen*

A Golden Legacy: Turmeric Across Time and Cultures

From the vibrant markets of Kerala to the serene rice terraces of Bali, turmeric's golden glow has been a constant thread in the fabric of human culture.

Turmeric, revered in Sanskrit as *Haridra*, has colored the lives of humans for more than 4,000 years. In classical Ayurvedic texts such as the *Sushruta Samhita* (circa 250 BCE), Haridra was revered for its wound-cleansing (*Vrana-shodhana*) and healing (*Vrana-ropana*) properties, often included in medicated ghee and oil formulations for ulcers and injuries (Bhishagratna, 1907).

By 700 AD, turmeric reached China; by 800 AD, East Africa; and by 1200 AD, West Africa. Along the Silk Road, it left a golden imprint on trade and culture. In 1280, Marco Polo described it as "a vegetable with all the properties of saffron"—a testament to its early global appeal (Polo, 1903).

Turmeric followed trade routes from India to Jamaica, embedding itself in cuisine and culture—an enduring symbol of sacredness, protection, and health.

From ancient Ayurvedic scrolls to today's scientific journals, turmeric impresses. It is no wonder the International Herb Association has crowned it the 2026 Herb of the Year. Wherever turmeric went, it left its golden fingerprint on skin, in healing, and across cultural traditions.

From Root to Remedy: Botany, Cultivation, and Harvest

Curcuma longa L., known by its synonyms *Curcuma domestica* and *Curcuma aromatica*, belongs to the Zingiberaceae family. This is the same botanical family that includes other notable plants like ginger *Zingiber officinale*, cardamom *Elettaria cardamomum*, galangal *Alpinia galanga*, and lesser-known allies such as *Kaempferia* and *Aframomum* species. *Curcuma longa* is the species name (genus + species), and the "L." in *Curcuma longa* L. represents Carl Linnaeus, the Swedish botanist who formalized the system of naming organisms, also known as binomial nomenclature, that we still use today.

Turmeric, also called Indian Saffron, at a spice market in India.
Dorene Petersen

Turmeric is a perennial herb that grows in graceful clusters. It reaches up to three feet tall with broad, emerald-green leaves unfurling from the base in elegant tufts. Pale yellow flowers emerge close to the ground, often nestled at the base of the foliage.

Beneath this leafy canopy, the real treasure takes shape: the rhizomes that branch and curl like golden fingers. The central rhizome tapers gently, typically two to three inches long, with smaller offshoots clustering around it. The rhizome has a brown exterior and a bright yellow to orange interior. When harvested, dried, and ground, these vibrant yellow-orange rhizomes transform into the familiar golden powder cherished across cultures. It has a warm, spicy fragrance and a pungent, slightly bitter taste. Note, while people often refer to "turmeric root" in casual language or marketing, "turmeric rhizome" is the botanically accurate term.

The common names include turmeric root, Indian saffron (remember what Marco Polo called it), curcuma, curcumin, and in herbal pharmacopoeias, it is known as *Curcumae longae rhizoma.*

Turmeric flourishes in tropical climates. In India, farmers know harvest time not by the calendar, but by the yellowing of leaves. Rhizomes are unearthed gently, dried, and often processed into powder or essential oil.

India supplies over 70% of the world's turmeric. Global demand is projected to reach $1 billion by 2030 (Kumar, 2025), offering opportunities and sustainability challenges for smallholder farmers. With the global market expected to grow 16% each year, India has a significant opportunity to scale up and lead the world in turmeric supply, benefiting farmers and the economy.

However, what does this mean on the ground?

For the individual farmer, turmeric is more than just a crop. It is a source of income, cultural identity, and resilience. Many smallholder farmers rely on turmeric as a cash crop. One that can be dried, stored, and sold when prices are best. With global demand on the rise and turmeric's reputation as a superfood still growing, each acre has the potential to bring real returns.

Explore an Indian turmeric field with this virtual field trip from ACHS's Indian study abroad tour on the ACHSTV YouTube channel: https://www.youtube.com/watch?v=Kkce00MZzro

Still, challenges remain, including climate unpredictability, fluctuating prices, and access to sustainable organic, pesticide-free growing practices. However, with proper support and fair-trade practices, the golden root can continue to uplift rural economies while feeding the world's growing appetite for wellness. When we source turmeric for our food and medicine, it is vital to consider the source and how we can support organic, sustainable practices, fair trade, and, ultimately, the well-being and lives of the families involved with growing and harvesting turmeric.

The Chemistry Behind the Gold: Constituents and Cultivars

Turmeric's magic lies in its chemistry. According to Abdel-Azim et al. (2020), the fresh turmeric rhizome contains 3–5% essential oil by weight, which is concentrated during steam distillation and is rich in sesquiterpene ketones like ar-turmerone and turmenone, along with aromatic compounds such as zingiberene, limonene, sabinene, ar-curcumene, 1,8-cineole, and bisabolene. These aromatic compounds are present in only trace amounts in the dried powder, which primarily retains curcuminoids like curcumin, demethoxycurcumin, and bisdemethoxycurcumin. It is important to distinguish between the therapeutic properties of the powdered rhizome and the essential oil. Achieving the therapeutic results you are looking for depends on this. To make it even more challenging, choosing the correct cultivar adds to successful results.

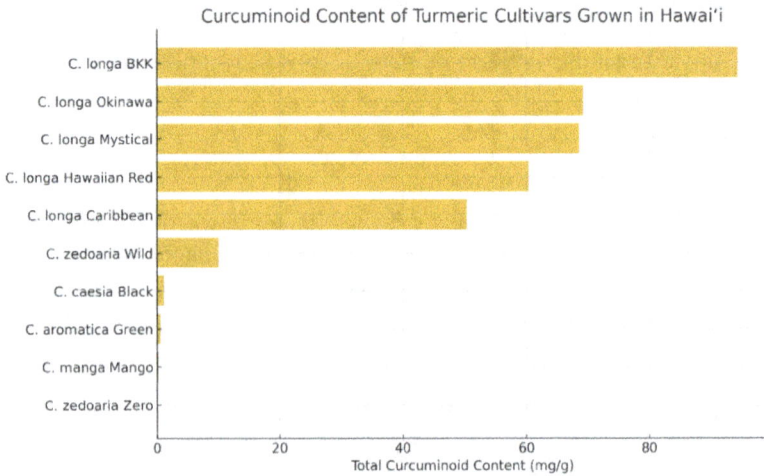

Curcuminoid Content of Turmeric Cultivars Grown in Hawai'i. *Chart by Matsuda & Chang.*

Place Matters: The Influence of Terroir on Turmeric's Potency

Turmeric's golden hue may be iconic, but its healing power depends on more than just color—it lies in the richness of its curcuminoids, particularly curcumin. To unlock its full therapeutic potential, it is essential to choose cultivars that are not only vibrant but also medicinally active.

In Hawai'i, HPLC analysis showed that visual color correlates with curcuminoid content. Cultivars like 'BKK' and 'Okinawa' yielded the highest levels, while paler varieties such as *C. zedoaria* showed little to none (Matsuda & Chang, 2021).

It is not just the species that shapes turmeric's therapeutic strength; just like a sought-after wine, where it is grown matters just as much. The *terroir*, or natural environment: soil, climate, and regional growing practices all imprint on the rhizome's chemistry.

Lawrence (2008) compared turmeric rhizome and tuber oils sourced from various growing regions and extracted by steam distillation and carbon dioxide (CO_2); the results revealed remarkable variation. One key compound—ar-turmerone—ranged from 1.65% to 24.87% depending on origin.

Perhaps even more surprising, the study found that CO_2 and steam-distilled oils had nearly identical chemical profiles. This challenged the long-held assumption that steam distillation fails to capture turmeric's full bouquet of constituents. Both methods proved capable of preserving turmeric's complex aromatic fingerprint.

Furthermore, it is not only the rhizome that holds healing potential. Turmeric's leaf oil, less commonly used but deeply promising, has demonstrated anti-inflammatory activity. Studies suggest its effects stem from its ability to modulate inflammatory pathways, including histamine, kinin1, and prostaglandins. It is another example of how every part of this plant offers something valuable, and how place, process, and plant work together harmoniously.

These results validate what traditional healers have long known: the visual cues of turmeric—the brightness, the depth of its gold—can guide us toward more potent, medicinally active varieties.

> In choosing turmeric, the eye is often the first tool of the herbalist, and the olfactory system is the first tool of the aromatherapist.

Clinical Promise: What Science Says Today

Today's research affirms the practices rooted in centuries of tradition. Turmeric supports the skin, joints, gut, bones, and brain.

A comprehensive 2024 review in *Pharmaceuticals* (Alam et al., 2024) examined curcumin's far-reaching therapeutic potential in conditions ranging from cancer and COVID-19 to diabetes, depression, arthritis, and Alzheimer's. Curcumin—found primarily in turmeric powder—demonstrated a powerful ability to calm inflammation, neutralize oxidative stress, and restore cellular balance. It acts on key signaling pathways like NF-κB, STAT3, and NLRP3, which are deeply involved in chronic disease processes. Its effects are not limited to inflammation; curcumin is also neuroprotective, antimicrobial, gut-calming, and anticancer. In clinical and animal studies, turmeric powder improved symptoms and reduced inflammation in ulcerative colitis, osteoarthritis, psoriasis, and metabolic syndrome—often with fewer side effects than conventional drugs.

The kinins are potent vasoactive basic peptides and their properties are wide ranging, including the ability to increase vascular permeability, cause vasodilation, pain, and the contraction of smooth muscle, and to stimulate arachidonic acid metabolism.

The following table provides a snapshot of how turmeric interacts with these three key pathways that influence inflammation and stress:

Table 1. How Turmeric Interacts with key pathways influencing inflammation and stress.

Pathway	What It Does	Why It Can Become a Problem	How Curcumin Supports
NF-κB (The Fire Alarm)	Triggers inflammation when the body senses injury or infection	Chronic inflammation when constantly activated	Reduces unnecessary inflammatory responses
STAT3 (The Growth Signal)	Tells cells to grow and divide	Overactive STAT3 is linked to pain, swelling, and even tumor growth	Helps regulate cell activity and restore balance
MAPK (The Stress Manager)	Coordinates cell response to stress, like irritation or damage	Can keep the stress/ inflammation cycle going if overactive	Calms stress responses, supporting tissue and skin repair

Why does this matter? By influencing these pathways, turmeric doesn't just mask symptoms; it helps reset the body's natural balance.

Turmeric essential oil, in contrast, contains virtually no curcumin. Instead, it is rich in volatile sesquiterpenes like ar-turmerone, α-turmerone, zingiberene, and 1,8-cineole. These compounds support anti-inflammatory, antimicrobial, and neuroregenerative activity, particularly through ar-turmerone's impact on neural stem cell proliferation. Leaf essential oil contains a slightly different chemical profile but shares many properties. Combined, the powder and essential oil may offer complementary benefits, addressing inflammation and oxidative stress through curcuminoids and volatile oils.

One major challenge with curcumin remains its poor bioavailability. Fortunately, recent advances in delivery—such as nanoparticle formulations, liposomal preparations, and pairing with piperine from black pepper—are dramatically improving absorption and clinical efficacy.

Choosing Between Turmeric Powder and Essential Oil

Each form of turmeric offers unique benefits. Use this quick reference to choose the best option based on your health goals.

Table 2. Comparison of Benefits of Turmeric Powder and Essential Oil.

Feature	Turmeric Powder	Turmeric Essential Oil
Main Constituents	Curcuminoids (Curcumin, Demethoxycurcumin, Bisdemethoxycurcumin)	Volatile sesquiterpenes (Ar-turmerone, α-/β-Turmerone, Zingiberene, 1,8-Cineole)
Primary Actions	Anti-inflammatory, Antioxidant, Anticancer, Neuroprotective	Anti-inflammatory, Antimicrobial, Neuroregenerative
Target Systems	Systemic: joints, gut, brain, metabolism, cardiovascular	Topical & neural: skin, brain, infections
Form Examples	Capsules, teas, food, standardized extracts	Essential oils, topical applications, diffusions, and enteric-coated capsules
Best Uses	Chronic inflammation, arthritis, colitis, neurodegenerative & metabolic conditions	Skin care, infections, cognitive support, adjunct to powder
Bioavailability	Low (enhanced with piperine, nanoparticles, liposomes)	Moderate (lipophilic, enhanced when combined with powder)

Cracking the Code: How Curcumin Calms Inflamed Skin

For centuries, turmeric has been revered in traditional medicine for its ability to soothe inflamed skin—from Ayurvedic preparations to Javanese bridal scrubs. Now, modern research is beginning to explain why it works so well.

Inflammatory skin conditions such as atopic dermatitis, and potentially eczema respond well to turmeric, and a recent 2025 study helps us understand the mechanism behind this. People with atopic conditions are said to have atopy, meaning their immune systems overreact to allergens, often producing high levels of IgE antibodies. This can lead to inflammation, itching, and hypersensitive skin or airways.

Researchers used network pharmacology and in vitro models to map curcumin's precise actions against skin inflammation. They found that curcumin interacts with major inflammation pathways, including NF-κB—the master switch for inflammation we discussed earlier—and MAPK. This key stress-response signal helps calm irritated skin at its root. This directly affects proteins involved in swelling, redness, and immune response. In lab tests on human skin cells, curcumin significantly reduced key markers of inflammation (Sureshbabu, Malarvizhi, Sivakumar, & Saravanan, 2025).

Sushruta's Compendium in 250 BCE was onto something when the authors recommended turmeric as a soothing ointment, applying turmeric to wounds and rashes. Fast forward to our modern lives—turmeric's relevance remains. See the chart below for practical guidance on dosage and administration for eczema and other inflammatory skin conditions.

Turmeric Dosage and Administration for Eczema, Dermatitis, and Other Inflammatory Skin Conditions.

Table 3. Turmeric Dosage and administration guidelines for inflammatory skin conditions

Route	Form	Dose	Frequency	Notes
Oral	Standardized curcumin extract (with piperine or phytosome)	500–2000 mg/day	1–2 times daily	Best taken with food and fat or black pepper to improve absorption
Topical	Turmeric-curcumin cream, gel, or oil-based preparation	0.5–3% curcumin	1–2 times daily	Do a patch test; it may cause temporary yellow staining of the skin

Always consult a qualified integrative healthcare provider before beginning herbal therapy.

Today's research increasingly supports what traditional healers have practiced for centuries: turmeric contributes to overall skin harmony, inside and out.

Turmeric for Joint Pain: A Natural Alternative to NSAIDs

Turmeric, long valued for its skin benefits, may also ease joint pain. Osteoarthritis of the knee— a common condition causing pain, stiffness, and swelling—has been the focus of several clinical studies on turmeric.

A 2014 randomized trial compared turmeric extract to ibuprofen in 367 patients with knee osteoarthritis. Participants took either 1,500 mg/day of turmeric extract or 1,200 mg/day of ibuprofen for four weeks. Results showed that turmeric was just as effective as ibuprofen in reducing pain and improving mobility, with the added benefit of fewer gastrointestinal side effects (Kuptniratsaikul et al., 2014).

More recently, a 2021 clinical study examined two traditional herbs— *Curcuma longa* (turmeric) and *Miconia albicans* (Canela de Velho)—for their ability to improve symptoms and reduce inflammation in osteoarthritis. Over 90 days, both herbs significantly reduced pain and stiffness, improved joint function, and lowered markers of inflammation in the blood. Importantly, turmeric was well tolerated, with no serious side effects (Gomes et al., 2021).

Research suggests *C. longa* primarily targets NF-κB and oxidative stress, while *Miconia albicans* has been shown to reduce pro-inflammatory cytokines and edema in preclinical arthritis models (Corrêa et al., 2021). Though no human studies have tested the two in combination, future research may reveal enhanced benefits for joint health when used together.

These findings reinforce what traditional healers have long known: turmeric can offer gentle yet meaningful relief from joint discomfort—an appealing option for those seeking alternatives to the long-term risks of NSAIDs.

Bone Healing and Beyond

Strong Roots: Turmeric and Bone Regeneration

Turmeric's healing powers may reach all the way to your bones. For centuries, turmeric has been used to promote healing and strength—and now science is confirming some of those traditional beliefs.

Osteoporosis

A clinical study looked at whether curcumin, the active compound in turmeric, could help women with osteoporosis when added to standard treatment (Khanizadeh, Gholami, Bagheri, & Dastani, 2018).

The study followed postmenopausal women for a year and compared three groups:

One group took calcium only.

The second group took alendronate, a common osteoporosis medication.

The third group took alendronate plus curcumin.

The study used 5 mg/day of alendronate, which is roughly equivalent to the commonly prescribed 35 mg/week or 70 mg/week doses used in osteoporosis treatment, and like Fosamax, alendronate is a bisphosphonate that slows bone breakdown.

The participants received 110 mg of curcumin per day in a nanomicellar, high-bioavailability formulation delivered in capsule form for oral use.

The results were striking. Women who combined curcumin with alendronate had the greatest improvement in bone density—even more than those who took alendronate alone. Bone strength improved at the spine, hip, and other key areas. Blood tests also showed healthier bone turnover, meaning more bone building and less bone breakdown. Best of all, there were no major side effects from adding curcumin.

What does this mean? Curcumin isn't a replacement for medication, but it may be a powerful partner for better bone health—especially when combined with standard treatment and used in a form your body can absorb well.

Osteoarthritis

In a recent preclinical study, curcumin significantly reduced bone loss and joint damage in a mouse model of osteoarthritis by inhibiting osteoclast activity in subchondral bone. These effects were linked to suppression of the NF-κB/JNK signaling pathway, which plays a central role in inflammation and bone resorption (Ding et al., 2024).

Fractures

This scientific insight echoes traditional use, where turmeric paste was applied to fractured limbs and golden milk was sipped to promote healing from within. Today, clinical research shows that curcumin—the active compound in turmeric—has been studied at daily doses ranging from 500 to 2,000 mg, often combined with piperine to enhance absorption in the body (Hewlings & Kalman, 2017).

Turmeric Meets Titanium: A New Frontier in Bone Healing

Peng, Tan, and Li (2025) demonstrated that curcumin-coated titanium surfaces enhanced stem cell adhesion and differentiation. Researchers found a new way to use turmeric's healing power on titanium dental and joint implants. In this study, scientists coated titanium surfaces with curcumin-loaded titanium dioxide nanotubes to help the body quickly accept and heal around the implants.

They tested these coated implants using advanced imaging and lab techniques. The results? The curcumin coatings did not just hold up—they also released the herb in a steady, controlled way and showed strong biocompatibility (meaning they are safe and friendly to living cells). When stem cells from rat bone marrow were added to the curcumin-coated surfaces, the cells grew better, attached well, and started turning into bone cells faster than on uncoated surfaces.

From Athlete's Foot to Agriculture: Turmeric's Role in Combating Fungi and Toxins

An older in vitro and in vivo study demonstrated that turmeric essential oil exhibits potent antifungal activity against *Trichophyton* species—a common cause of athlete's foot (tinea pedis) and ringworm. The essential oil also effectively treated *Trichophyton*-induced dermatophytosis in guinea pigs, confirming its traditional use for fungal skin infections (Apisariyakul et al., 1995).

Both turmeric essential oil and curcumin have been shown to suppress the growth of harmful molds such as *Aspergillus flavus* and inhibit aflatoxin production. Sidhu et al. (2011) demonstrated that turmeric leaf oil blocked fungal growth and aflatoxins (B_1 and G_1) formation in vitro, achieving up to 100% inhibition at higher concentrations. Ferreira et al. (2013) found that turmeric rhizome oil and curcumin reduced aflatoxin production by more than 96% at 0.5%.

Research continues with the promise of a new era in food technology. Turmeric is not just healing people—it may soon help protect our food supply. In a cutting-edge study (Murugesan et al., 2023), encapsulated turmeric essential oil—rich in aromatic compounds like α-turmerone, β-turmerone, and 1,8-cineole- within chitosan nanoparticles, was found to be a safe, food-grade biopolymer. The nano-encapsulated oil demonstrated strong antimicrobial action against foodborne pathogens (*Staphylococcus aureus, Pseudomonas aeruginosa*), completely inhibited mold growth and mycotoxin production (zearalenone and deoxynivalenol) by *Fusarium graminearum*, showed robust antioxidant activity, and did not harm seed germination—suggesting crop-safe application in sustainable food preservation (Murugesan et al., 2023).

This study does not just confirm turmeric's traditional antimicrobial power—it reimagines it for the future of food safety and sustainable agriculture.

Turmeric and Cancer: What the Science Shows

Turmeric has long been used to support the body during illness, but now, research suggests that curcumin, the bright yellow compound in turmeric, may help fight cancer in powerful ways.

Early research from Louisiana State University showed that curcumin could slow the growth of specific cancer cells, including rhabdomyosarcoma, a type of soft tissue cancer, by stopping them early in their life cycle and blocking key signals that tell tumors to grow (Beevers, Huang, & Lee, 2006).

Since then, studies have continued to explore how curcumin works. Scientists have found that curcumin targets many of the same pathways which cancer cells use to survive, spread, and resist treatment. It has been shown to:

Slow the growth of tumors (Park et al., 2020)

Help cancer cells self-destruct naturally (*The Bright Side of Curcumin*, 2024)

Prevent new blood vessels from feeding tumors (Frontiers et al., 2022)

Reduce inflammation that can fuel cancer (Curran et al., 2024)

In breast, colon, lung, prostate, and pancreatic cancers, curcumin has shown encouraging results in both lab and early clinical studies. Some trials have even found that curcumin, when taken alongside chemotherapy, can make treatment more effective and less toxic (MDPI Review Team, 2023).

Moreover, with new forms of curcumin like nanoparticles and enhanced capsules, researchers are improving its bioavailability, helping the body absorb more curcumin and deliver it to where it is needed most (Bertoncini-Silva et al., 2024). Note: An enhanced capsule is a curcumin supplement specially designed for better absorption. It often uses tiny fat-based carriers or nanoparticles, so more curcumin gets into your bloodstream and reaches the areas where it's needed most.

While turmeric is not a cancer cure, its ability to support the body and complement current medical treatment makes it a valuable addition to the conversation around integrative cancer care.

Turmeric and Colon Health: Clinical Evidence Emerges

A 2022 randomized, placebo-controlled trial published in *Genes* investigated whether a turmeric-based supplement could help people with familial adenomatous polyposis (FAP)—a rare genetic disorder in which hundreds of polyps develop in the colon, increasing cancer risk.

Participants took capsules containing curcumin, turmerones, ginger, seaweed, and black pepper for six months—a blend inspired by traditional use.

What did the researchers find?

Overall, turmeric did not significantly reduce the total number of polyps across the colon. However, promising trends appeared in the left colon: in some participants, polyp numbers dropped from about five to one or two, and total size decreased by more than half. Aside from mild stomach upset in a few cases, no serious side effects occurred (Gilad et al., 2022).

Although the overall results were not statistically significant, these subgroup findings suggest that turmeric, especially when combined with other supportive herbs, may have a role in protecting colon health. They also raise an intriguing question: Does turmeric work better in certain parts of the colon?

More research is needed, but this trial represents an important step in understanding turmeric's potential role in colon wellness.

Turmeric and the Aging Brain: What the Science Shows

Turmeric has long been valued in traditional medicine as a brain tonic to sharpen the mind and calm the body. Today, modern research is starting to validate those claims.

A 2025 systematic review and meta-analysis of nine randomized controlled trials involving 501 participants examined curcumin, turmeric's best-known active compound, for its role in cognitive aging (Wang et al., 2025).

The results? While curcumin did not dramatically boost overall cognition, the analysis found modest but significant improvements in working memory and processing speed, particularly in studies lasting at least 24 weeks and using enhanced formulations such as nanoparticles or micelles. Some trials also reported better mood and attention.

Side effects were mild, mostly digestive discomfort at higher doses. The key challenge is bioavailability—curcumin in its natural form is poorly absorbed, so specialized delivery systems or piperine combinations are essential for clinical benefit.

Although curcumin is not a cure for Alzheimer's or cognitive decline, this evidence suggests it may be a useful ally for long-term brain health, especially when taken in bioavailable form.

Turmeric Dosage, Cautions, and Regulatory Status

How Much to Take: Traditional Guidance Meets Modern Use

Turmeric has been used safely for centuries. What do current research and traditional use suggest as safe dosages? The answer depends on the form.

Standardized supplements are often chosen over teas or powders because curcumin and other active compounds have low bioavailability. Advanced formulations—like those combined with black pepper or liposomes—can dramatically improve absorption.

Common Daily Dosages

Table 4. Dosage comparison chart based on preparation form.

Preparation Form	Dosage	Source(s)
Powdered Root	0.5–1 g between meals, up to 3 g/day	EMA (2018), Hewlings & Kalman (2017), Kunnumakkara et al. (2017)
Fluid Extract (1:1)	1–3 mL per day	EMA (2018)
Tincture (1:5 in 60% alcohol)	2–4 mL per day	EMA (2018)
Essential oil	1 drop (0.03–0.05 mL) daily of certified organic, pesticide-free steam-distilled oil, diluted in a food-grade base oil.[1]	Joshi et al. (2003)

This represents a highly conservative dosage compared to clinically tested amounts. In a phase I safety trial, healthy volunteers tolerated oral turmeric oil at much higher levels—0.6 mL three times daily for one month, escalating to 1 mL three times daily for two months—without serious adverse effects (Joshi et al., 2003*). Note: internal use of essential oils is not widely endorsed without supervision and should be professionally guided. This is for informational purposes only and not a recommendation for self-use.*

Depending on the desired support, these forms are often combined, whether for digestion, inflammation, skin, or overall vitality.

Cautions and Considerations

Turmeric and its constituents are generally well tolerated when used within recommended dosages, and it has a long history of culinary and therapeutic use. However, certain conditions require caution or professional supervision.

Pregnancy and Lactation

While culinary use of turmeric is considered safe during pregnancy, high doses and concentrated extracts are traditionally avoided due to potential uterine-stimulating effects (Dugoua et al., 2008). Limited clinical data exist; therefore, individuals who are pregnant or lactating should seek guidance from a qualified healthcare practitioner before using turmeric in medicinal amounts.

Gallbladder Disorders

Turmeric exhibits choleretic activity, stimulating bile flow (Rafatullah et al., 1990). Individuals with gallstones, bile duct obstruction, or gallbladder inflammation should avoid therapeutic doses unless under medical supervision.

Bleeding and Surgery

Curcumin may have mild antiplatelet activity and could slow blood clotting, potentially increasing bleeding risk (Chainani-Wu, 2003). Turmeric should be used with caution by individuals taking anticoagulants or antiplatelet medications (e.g., warfarin, aspirin, clopidogrel, rivaroxaban) and discontinued at least two weeks prior to surgery.

Diabetes

Curcuminoids may lower blood glucose levels by enhancing glucose transporter activity (Den Hartogh et al., 2020). People using insulin or oral hypoglycemic medications should monitor their blood sugar closely and consult their healthcare provider before adding turmeric supplements.

Iron Absorption

Turmeric may reduce non-heme iron absorption, potentially contributing to iron deficiency in susceptible individuals (Tripathi & Misra, 1974). Those with anemia or low ferritin levels should avoid high doses or take turmeric separately from iron supplements.

Hormone-Sensitive Conditions

While curcumin does not act as a phytoestrogen, some practitioners recommend caution in individuals with hormone-sensitive conditions, such as breast, ovarian, or uterine cancers, until further research clarifies its effects (Goel et al., 2008).

Skin Sensitivity

Rare cases of contact dermatitis have been reported, primarily from topical application of turmeric or curcumin (Goel et al., 2008). Oral use rarely causes hypersensitivity reactions.

Turmeric remains a safe and versatile botanical when used responsibly. However, individuals with the above conditions should exercise caution and seek professional guidance before using concentrated extracts or essential oils.

Regulatory Status

Turmeric enjoys widespread legal acceptance globally, but regulations vary by region:

United States: Turmeric and its preparations hold GRAS (Generally Recognized As Safe) status as a food ingredient. Turmeric is regulated under the Dietary Supplement Health and Education Act (DSHEA, 1994) as a dietary supplement. Supplements must not claim to treat, cure, or prevent disease and must carry the FDA-mandated disclaimer: *"This statement has not been evaluated by the FDA..."* (FDA, 2023).

European Union (EU): Turmeric (*Curcuma longa* rhizome) is listed in the European Medicines Agency (EMA) Herbal Monograph, in-dicated for mild digestive disorders. It is regulated as a traditional herbal medicinal product under Directive 2004/24/EC. Oral essential oil use is not authorized for self-care (EMA, 2018).

Canada: Turmeric is classified as a Natural Health Product (NHP) by Health Canada. Permissible claims include "Used in Herbal Medicine as an anti-inflammatory to help relieve joint pain." Products must have an NPN (Natural Product Number) and comply with quality and evidence standards (Health Canada, 2022)

Australia: Under the Therapeutic Goods Administration (TGA), turmeric is listed as a complementary medicine. Approved indications include relief of mild digestive disturbances and joint inflammation. All products must meet Good Manufacturing Practice (GMP) and labeling standards (TGA, 2023).

India: Turmeric is regulated under Ayush systems and widely used in Ayurvedic formulations. Both raw turmeric and standardized extracts are permitted for internal and external use under Ayur-vedic Pharmacopoeia standards (Government of India, 2021).

WHO: The WHO Monograph on *Curcuma longa* recognizes its use for digestive and liver support, limits therapeutic doses, and recommends caution in pregnancy and gallbladder disease (WHO, 2019).

Bioavailability Tip: Getting the Most Benefits from Turmeric

Turmeric is powerful—but only if your body can absorb it! Curcumin, its active compound, has low natural bioavailability, meaning most of it passes through without being used. Following are tips to unlock its full healing potential; you'll also find these ingredients incorporated in my formulas.

Pair it with black pepper (piperine): Boosts absorption by up to 2000% by slowing curcumin's breakdown.

Take it with healthy fats: Curcumin is fat-soluble and better absorbed by oils like olive, coconut, or avocado.

Look for enhanced formulations: Modern options like phospholipid-bound, liposomal, or nanoparticle curcumin are designed for better delivery to your cells.

Do not rely on plain turmeric powder alone: While useful in food, it does not deliver high enough doses of curcumin for therapeutic use (Hewlings & Kalman, 2017). Choose a high-quality curcumin supplement with absorption-enhancing features for best results—and take it with a meal containing healthy fats.

Nourish & Heal: Turmeric Formulations for Mind and Body

Explore these versatile turmeric-inspired blends designed to add warmth, balance, and harmony to your self-care rituals.

Spice of Life Massage Oil

An aromatic blend that brings a warm, uplifting, and balancing touch to your massage experience.

6 drops Ginger *Zingiber officinale* oil
6 drops Ylang ylang *Cananga odorata* oil
4 drops Coriander *Coriandrum sativum* oil
4 drops Turmeric *Curcuma longa* oil

To prepare the massage oil with a 2% dilution, measure 1 ounce (30 mL) of apricot kernel oil (or another preferred carrier). Add 10 to 12 drops of the Spice of Life Blend. Mix gently and store in a dark glass bottle. Perform a skin patch test before use, then apply to the desired areas.

Golden Wellness Massage Oil

While the Spice of Life blend offers a vibrant, energizing feel, the Golden Wellness formula is formulated to support relaxation and calm through a combination of grounding and harmonizing essential oils.

6 drops Frankincense *Boswellia carterii*
5 drops Lavender *Lavandula angustifolia*
4 drops Marjoram *Origanum majorana*
3 drops Turmeric *Curcuma longa*

To prepare the massage oil with a 2% dilution, measure 1 ounce (30 mL) of apricot kernel oil (or substitute with jojoba, sweet almond, or grapeseed oil). Add 10 to 12 drops of the Golden Wellness essential oil blend. Cap tightly and swirl or roll the bottle gently to mix. Store in a dark glass bottle, away from heat and sunlight. Perform a skin patch test before use, then massage onto sore muscles or tension points.

Ease & Flow Massage Oil

A comforting, herbaceous blend with soft, woody undertones, ideal for moments when you crave deep relaxation.

5 drops Marjoram *Origanum majorana*
3 drops Rosemary *Rosmarinus officinalis*
1 drop Chamomile Roman *Chamaemelum nobile*
1 drop Turmeric *Curcuma longa*

To prepare the massage oil with a 2% dilution, measure 1 ounce (30 mL) of a carrier oil such as apricot kernel, jojoba, or sweet almond oil. Add the entire Ease & Flow Blend (10 drops total) to the carrier oil. Cap tightly and swirl gently to combine. Store in a dark glass bottle, away from heat and sunlight. Perform a skin patch test before use, then massage onto inflamed or sore joints, strained muscles, or areas of back pain.

Natural Turmeric Skin Cream
(Oil Infusion Method)

A rich, nurturing, calming, brightening cream infused with turmeric's golden essence, offering a soft, silky finish for everyday skin indulgence.

5 grams turmeric powder organic *Curcuma longa*
100 mL carrier oil: jojoba *Simmondsia chinensis*, almond *Prunus amygdalus dulcis*, or sunflower *Helianthus annuus*
18 grams candelilla wax *Euphorbia cerifera*
10 grams shea butter *Vitellaria paradoxa* or lanolin
20 mL distilled water
7 mL glycerin, vegetable-derived
1 gram borax natural stabilizer
Few drops essential oil (optional, e.g., lavender *Lavandula angustifolia*)
Natural preservative, e.g., vitamin E *Tocopherol*, or leucidal liquid, as directed

To infuse the oil, combine turmeric powder and carrier oil in a clean glass jar. Infuse in a warm, dark place for 2 to 3 weeks, shaking daily. Strain through cheesecloth to obtain turmeric-infused oil.

To prepare the oil phase, gently melt candelilla wax and shea butter in a double boiler. Stir in turmeric-infused oil until thoroughly blended.

To prepare the water phase, heat distilled water, glycerin, and borax together to ~70°C (158°F)

To combine, slowly add the oil phase into the water phase while whisking to emulsify.

Cool to ~ 40°C (104°F), then add essential oils and preservative.

Add a few drops of essential oil, optional, and mix gently to incorporate.

Add your chosen preservative and mix thoroughly to ensure even distribution: Vitamin E (*Tocopherol*): 0.5 to 1% of total formula (10 to 20 drops or 0.5 to 1 gram per 100 g cream) or leucidal liquid: typically, 2 to 4% of total formula (about 2 to 4 gram per 100 gram cream).

Pour the finished cream into sterilized glass jars, cover tightly, and allow to set for 24 hours.

Note: a preservative is essential for emulsions containing water to prevent microbial growth and extend shelf life. Store in a cool place. Always perform a skin patch test before use, especially for turmeric sensitivity.

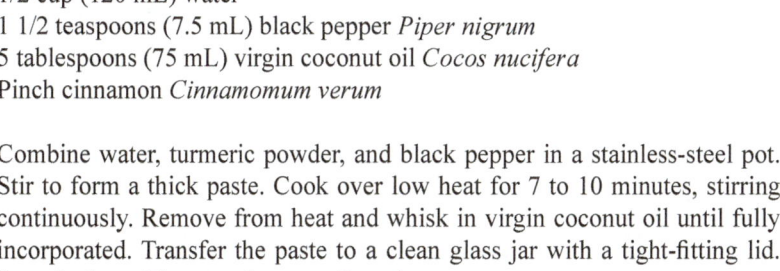

Golden Paste for Golden Milk

A golden-hued paste that transforms warm milk into a cozy, aromatic drink with subtle spice notes.

1/2 cup (120 mL) organic turmeric powder *Curcuma longa*
1/2 cup (120 mL) water
1 1/2 teaspoons (7.5 mL) black pepper *Piper nigrum*
5 tablespoons (75 mL) virgin coconut oil *Cocos nucifera*
Pinch cinnamon *Cinnamomum verum*

Combine water, turmeric powder, and black pepper in a stainless-steel pot. Stir to form a thick paste. Cook over low heat for 7 to 10 minutes, stirring continuously. Remove from heat and whisk in virgin coconut oil until fully incorporated. Transfer the paste to a clean glass jar with a tight-fitting lid. Store in the refrigerator for up to 2 weeks.

To prepare Golden Milk, whisk one teaspoon (5 mL) of Golden Paste into 2 cups (480 mL) of warm milk (dairy or plant-based). Sweeten with raw honey, molasses, or a pinch of cinnamon to taste. Black pepper and coconut oil enhance curcumin absorption.

Golden Synergy Oil

A smooth, golden oil featuring turmeric and warming spices, perfect for enhancing culinary creations or blending into your favorite warm beverage.

1/2 cup (120mL) organic coconut oil or MCT oil
1 tablespoon (15mL) organic turmeric powder *Curcuma longa*
1/4 teaspoon (1.25 mL) black pepper *Piper nigrum* (freshly ground)

Warm coconut or MCT oil on low heat (do not boil). Stir in turmeric powder and black pepper until thoroughly blended. Remove from heat and cool slightly. Pour into a dark glass jar and cap tightly. Shake gently before each use. Store in a cool, dark place. Use within 3 weeks.

Take one teaspoon (5 mL) daily with food. May be stirred into warm milk, dairy or plant-based.

The Golden Takeaway

Whether sipped in warm milk, blended into nourishing oils, or diffused into the air, turmeric remains a golden ally—linking ancient wisdom with modern science and honoring the earth's healing power. Sip, blend, breathe, and glow—let turmeric guide you on your path to wellness.

Glossary

NF-κBs: NF-κB (short for nuclear factor kappa-light-chain-enhancer of activated B cells) is like a master switch inside your cells that controls inflammation. When your body is under stress—from injury, infection, or even chronic disease—NF-κB turns on and tells your cells to produce inflammatory chemicals. This is helpful in the short term (like healing a cut), but when NF-κB stays switched on too long, it can lead to chronic inflammation, pain, swelling, and tissue damage—especially in conditions like arthritis, eczema, or autoimmune disorders.

Many herbs, including turmeric, help calm NF-κB down, which is one reason they're so effective for managing inflammation naturally.

NLRP3: NLRP3 stands for NOD-like receptor pyrin domain 3. It's like an internal smoke detector in your immune system that triggers inflammation when it senses danger. When overactive, it can lead to chronic inflammation and disease.

PGE_2: PGE_2 is a chemical signal your body makes during inflammation. It helps trigger pain, swelling, and fever to start healing—but too much can cause chronic pain and tissue damage. Curcumin helps reduce PGE_2, easing inflammation.

RANKL: RANKL is a signal that tells special cells (osteoclasts) to break down bone. It's needed for normal bone renewal, but too much RANKL causes bone loss and weak bones. Curcumin helps lower RANKL, supporting bone strength.

STAT3: STAT3 (short for Signal Transducer and Activator of Transcription 3) is like a cellular messenger that helps your body respond to stress, inflammation, and injury.

When something goes wrong—like an infection, inflammation, or cancer—STAT3 can become overly active and tell cells to grow, divide, or produce more inflammation than necessary. This can cause problems like chronic swelling, joint pain, or even support the growth of tumors.

Turmeric, especially curcumin, has been shown to calm down STAT3 when it's overactive, helping reduce inflammation and support your body's return to balance.

References

Abdel-Azim, N. S., Shabana, M. M., Ali, A. A., El Sayed, A. M., & Sleem, A. A. (2020). "Curcuma longa L. rhizome essential oil: A review of extraction, chemical composition, and biological effects." *Plants*, 10(1), 44. Retrieved May 16, 2025. https://www.mdpi.com/2223-7747/10/1/44.

Alam, M. S., Anwar, M. J., Maity, M. K., Azam, F., Jaremko, M., & Emwas, A.-H. (2024). "The Dynamic Role of Curcumin in Mitigating Human Illnesses: Recent Advances in Therapeutic Applications." *Pharmaceuticals*, *17*(12), 1674. Retrieved May 16, 2025, https://doi.org/10.3390/ph17121674.

Apisariyakul, A., Vanittanakom, N., & Buddhasukh, D. (1995). "Antifungal activity of turmeric oil extracted from Curcuma longa (Zingiberaceae)." *Journal of Ethnopharmacology*, 49(3), 163–169. Retrieved May 26, 2025. https://www.sciencedirect.com/science/article/abs/pii/0378874195013202?via%3Dihub.

Beevers, C. S., Huang, S., & Lee, S. H. (2006). "Curcumin inhibits the mammalian target of rapamycin-mediated signaling pathways in rhabdomyosarcoma cells." *Cancer Research*, 66(3), 1615–1621. Retrieved June 5, 2025. https://pubmed.ncbi.nlm.nih.gov/16550606/.

Bertoncini-Silva, C., Vlad, A., Ricciarelli, R., et al. (2024). "Enhancing the bioavailability and bioactivity of curcumin for disease prevention and treatment." *Antioxidants, 13*(3), 331. https://doi.org/10.3390/antiox13030331 Retrieved July 24, 2025. PubMed: https://pubmed.ncbi.nlm.nih.gov/38539864.

Bhishagratna, K. L. (1907). "An English translation of the Sushruta Samhita based on the original Sanskrit text." (Vol. I). Calcutta: [Publisher not clearly stated, historical edition]. Retrieved July 24, 2025. https://rarebooksocietyofindia.org/book_archive/Sushruta%20Samhita%201.pdf.

Chainani-Wu, N. (2003). "Safety and anti-inflammatory activity of curcumin: A component of turmeric (Curcuma longa)." *The Journal of Alternative and Complementary Medicine*, 9(1), 161–168. https://doi.org/10.1089/107555303321223035. Retrieved July 29, 2025. https://www.liebertpub.com/doi/10.1089/107555303321223035.

Corrêa, J. G. de S., Bianchin, M., Lopes, A. P., Silva, E., Ames, F. Q., Pomini, A. M., Carpes, S. T., Rinaldi, J. de C., Melo, R. C., Kioshima, E. S., Bersani-Amado, C. A., Pilau, E. J., de Carvalho, J. E., Ruiz, A. L. T. G., & Santin, S. M. de O. (2021). "Chemical profile, antioxidant and anti-inflammatory properties of *Miconia albicans* (Sw.) Triana (Melastomataceae) fruits extract." *Journal of Ethnopharmacology, 273*, 113979. https://doi.org/10.1016/j.jep.2021.113979 Retrieved July 21, 2025.

https://www.sciencedirect.com/science/article/pii/S0378874121002063.

Curran, M. P., Sharma, S., Patel, G., et al. (2024). "Curcumin in cancer and inflammation: molecular mechanisms and clinical insights." *International Journal of Molecular Sciences*, 25(9), 5001. https://doi.org/10.3390/ijms25095001 Retrieved July 08 2025. https://www.mdpi.com/1422-0067/25/9/5001.

Den Hartogh, D. J., Gabriel, A., & Tsiani, E. (2020). "Antidiabetic Properties of Curcumin I: Evidence from In Vitro Studies." *Nutrients,* 12(1), 118. https://doi.org/10.3390/nu12010118 Retrieved July 24, 2025. PubMed: https://pubmed.ncbi.nlm.nih.gov/31906278.

Ding, D., Liu, G., Yan, J., Zhang, Q., Meng, F., & Wang, L. (2024). "Curcumin alleviates osteoarthritis in mice by suppressing osteoclastogenesis in subchondral bone via inhibiting NFκB/JNK signaling pathway." PLOS ONE, 19(9), e0309807. https://doi.org/10.1371/journal.pone.0309807 Retrieved May 15, 2025. https://journals.plos.org/plosone/article?id=10.1371/journal.pone.0309807.

Dugoua, J. J., Seely, D., Perri, D., Cooley, K., Forelli, T., Mills, E., & Koren, G. (2008). "Safety and efficacy of turmeric (Curcuma longa) during pregnancy and lactation." *Canadian Journal of Clinical Pharmacology*, 15(1), e66–e73. Retrieved July 27, 2025. https://www.researchgate.net/publication/23700343.

European Medicines Agency. (2018). "Assessment report on *Curcuma longa* L., rhizoma." EMA/HMPC/150777/2015. Retrieved May 08, 2025. https://www.ema.europa.eu/en/documents/herbal-report/draft-assessment-report-curcuma-longa-l-c-domestica-valeton-rhizome-revision-1_en.pdf.

Ferreira, F. D., Kemmelmeier, C., Arrotéia, C. C., da Costa, C. L., Mallmann, C. A., & Machinski Jr., M. (2013). "Inhibitory effect of the essential oil of Curcuma longa L. and curcumin on aflatoxin production by Aspergillus flavus Link." *Food Chemistry*, 136(2), 789–793. https://doi.org/10.1016/j.foodchem.2012.08.003. Retrieved July 13, 2025. https://www.sciencedirect.com/science/article/abs/pii/S0308814612012465.

Food and Drug Administration (FDA). (2023). *Dietary supplement labeling guide.* Retrieved May 02, 2025. https://www.fda.gov/food/dietary-supplements.

Gilad, O., Rosner, G., Ivancovsky-Wajcman, D., Zur, R., Rosin-Arbesfeld, R., Gluck, N., Strul, H., Lehavi, D., Rolfe, V., & Kariv, R. (2022). "Efficacy of Wholistic Turmeric Supplement on Adenomatous Polyps in Patients with Familial Adenomatous Polyposis: A randomized, double-blinded, placebo-controlled study." *Genes*, 13(12), 2182. Retrieved June 04, 2025. https://www.mdpi.com/2073-4425/13/12/2182.

Goel, A., Kunnumakkara, A. B., & Aggarwal, B. B. (2008). "Curcumin as 'Curecumin': From kitchen to clinic." *Biochemical Pharmacology*, 75(4), 787–809. https://doi.org/10.1016/j.bcp.2007.08.016. Retrieved June 04, 2025. https://www.sciencedirect.com/science/article/abs/pii/S0006295207005758?via%3Dihub.

Gomes, T. P. O., Souza, J. I. N., Somerlate, L. C., Mendonça, V. A., Lima, N. M., Carli, G. P., Castro, S. B. R., Andrade, T. J. A. S., Dias, J. V. L., Oliveira, M. A. L., Alves, C. C. S., & Carli, A. P. (2021). "Miconia albicans and Curcuma longa herbal medicines positively modulate joint pain, function, and inflammation in patients with osteoarthritis: A clinical study." *Inflammopharmacology*, 29, 617–626.Retrieved June 04, 2025. https://pubmed.ncbi.nlm.nih.gov/33452967/.

Government of India. (2021). *Ayurvedic Pharmacopoeia of India*. Retrieved July 25, 2025. https://www.ayush.gov.in.

Health Canada. (2022). *Natural health products: Ingredient database*. Retrieved May 03, 2025. https://www.canada.ca.

Hewlings, S. J., & Kalman, D. S. (2017). "Curcumin: A review of its effects on human health. Foods." 6(10), 92. Retrieved June 04, 2025. https://pmc.ncbi.nlm.nih.gov/articles/PMC5664031/.

Joshi, J., Ghaisas, S., Vaidya, A., Vaidya, R., Kamat, D. V., Bhagwat, A. N., & Bhide, S. (2003). "Early human safety study of turmeric oil (Curcuma longa oil) administered orally in healthy volunteers." *Journal of the Association of Physicians of India*, 51, 1055–1060. Retrieved May 01, 2025. https://pubmed.ncbi.nlm.nih.gov/15260388.

Khanizadeh, F., Rahmani, A., Asadollahi, K., & Ahmadi, M. R. H. (2018). "Combination therapy of curcumin and alendronate modulates bone turnover markers and enhances bone mineral density in postmenopausal women with osteoporosis." *Archives of endocrinology and metabolism*, 62(4), 438–445. Retrieved July 24, 2025. https://doi.org/10.20945/2359-3997000000060.

Kunnumakkara, A. B., Bordoloi, D., Padmavathi, G., Monisha, J., Roy, N. K., Prasad, S., & Aggarwal, B. B. (2017). "Curcumin, the golden nutraceutical: Multitargeting for multiple chronic diseases." *British Journal of Pharmacology*, 174(11), 1325–1348. Retrieved July 24, 2025. https://doi.org/10.1111/bph.13621.

Kuptniratsaikul, V., Thanakhumtorn, S., Chinswangwatanakul, P., Wattanamongkonsil, L., & Thamlikitkul, V. (2014). "Efficacy and safety of Curcuma domestica extracts compared with ibuprofen in patients with knee osteoarthritis." *Clinical Interventions in Aging*, 9, 451–458. https://doi.

org/10.2147/CIA.S58535 Retrieved July 24, 2025. PubMed: https://pubmed.ncbi.nlm.nih.gov/24672232.

Lawrence, B. M. (2008). "Variations in turmeric oil composition from different growing regions." *Perfumer & Flavorist*, 33, 32–39. Retrieved July 19, 2025. https://www.perfumerflavorist.com/flavor/ingredients/article/21860830/progress-in-essential-oils-turmeric-oil-part-1.

Matsuda, S., & Chang, C. (2021). "Curcuminoid content of turmeric cultivars in Hawaii." *Journal of Medicinal Plants Research*, 15(3), 45–52. Retrieved June 20, 2025. https://gms.ctahr.hawaii.edu/gs/handler/getmedia.ashx?moid=29948&dt=3&g=12.

MDPI Review Team. (2023). "Curcumin enhances the efficacy of doxorubicin, paclitaxel, 5fluorouracil, and cisplatin in preclinical breast cancer models: mechanisms and potential for combinational therapy." *International Journal of Molecular Sciences*, 23(4), 2144. https://doi.org/10.3390/ijms23042144 Retrieved July 09, 2025. https://www.mdpi.com/1422-0067/23/4/2144.

Murugesan, S., Rajkumar, V., Annapoorani, C. A., & Gunasekaran, C. (2023). "Functionalized nanoencapsulated *Curcuma longa* essential oil in chitosan nanopolymer and their application for antioxidant and antimicrobial efficacy." *International Journal of Biological Macromolecules*, 251, 126387. Retrieved May 12, 2025. https://doi.org/10.1016/j.ijbiomac.2023.126387.

Peng, H., Tan, J., & Li, X. (2025). "Loading curcumin on TiO_2 nanotubes to improve surface biological activity." *Biomedical Materials*, 20(4). Retrieved June 15th, 2025. https://doi.org/10.1088/1748-605X/ade488.

Polo, M. (1903). *The book of Ser Marco Polo, the Venetian: Concerning the kingdoms and marvels of the East.* (H. Yule & H. Cordier, Eds., Vol. 2). London: John Murray. Retrieved June 15th, 2025. https://www.gutenberg.org/files/12410/12410-h/12410-h.htm.

Rafatullah, S., Tariq, M., Al-Yahya, M. A., Mossa, J. S., & Ageel, A. M. (1990). "Evaluation of turmeric (Curcuma longa) for gastric and duodenal antiulcer activity in rats." *Journal of Ethnopharmacology*, 29(1), 25–34. https://doi.org/10.1016/0378-8741(90)90018-B. Retrieved July 01, 2025. https://www.sciencedirect.com/science/article/abs/pii/037887419090094A.

Shoba, G., Joy, D., Joseph, T., Majeed, M., Rajendran, R., & Srinivas, P. S. (1998). "Influence of piperine on the pharmacokinetics of curcumin in animals and human volunteers." *Planta medica*, *64*(4), 353–356. Retrieved July 20th, 2025. https://doi.org/10.1055/s-2006-957450.

Sidhu, S., Chempakam, B., Leela, N. K., & Bhai, R. S. (2011).

"Chemoprevention by essential oil of turmeric leaves (Curcuma longa L.) on the growth of Aspergillus flavus and aflatoxin production." *Food and Chemical Toxicology*, 49(5), 1188–1192. https://doi.org/10.1016/j.fct.2011.02.014. Retrieved May 04, 2025. https://pubmed.ncbi.nlm.nih.gov/21354246/.

Sureshbabu, S., Malarvizhi, G. L., Sivakumar, K., & Saravanan, M. (2025). "Unraveling the molecular mechanism of curcumin against atopic dermatitis: An integration of network pharmacology, molecular docking, and in vitro validation." *Drug Development Research*. Advance online publication. https://doi.org/10.1002/ddr.70058 Retrieved June 15th, 2025. https://analyticalsciencejournals.onlinelibrary.wiley.com/doi/10.1002/ddr.70058.

Therapeutic Goods Administration (TGA). (2023). *Permissible indications for listed medicines*. Retrieved June 06, 2025, https://www.tga.gov.au.

"The Bright Side of Curcumin: A Narrative Review of Its Therapeutic Potential in Cancer." (2024). *Cancers*, 16(14), 2580. Retrieved July 29, 2025. https://www.mdpi.com/2072-6694/16/14/2580.

Tripathi, R., & Misra, R. (1974). "Effect of turmeric and its curcuminoids on iron absorption in rats." *Indian Journal of Medical Research*, 62(3), 436–441. Retrieved June 27, 2025. https://pubmed.ncbi.nlm.nih.gov/4415866.

Wang, W., Zhao, R., Liu, B., & Li, K. (2025). "The effect of curcumin supplementation on cognitive function: An updated systematic review and meta-analysis." *Frontiers in Nutrition*, eCollection 2025. Retrieved July 24, 2025. https://doi.org/10.3389/fnut.2025.1549509.

World Health Organization (WHO). (2019). "WHO monographs on selected medicinal plants – Curcuma longa." Retrieved June 16, 2025. https://iris.who.int/bitstream/handle/10665/42052/9241545178.pdf.

Yu, L., Li, N., Li, B., Ye, K. X., Guo, J., Shan, J., Cao, L., Song, M., Wang, Y., Lee, T. S., Maier, A. B., & Feng, L. (2025). "Targeting cognitive aging with curcumin supplementation: A systematic review and meta-analysis." *The Journal of Prevention of Alzheimer's Disease*, 100248. Advance online publication. Retrieved June 21, 2025, https://pubmed.ncbi.nlm.nih.gov/40579315/.

Zhou J, Wang L, Peng C and Peng F (2022) "Co-Targeting Tumor Angiogenesis and Immunosuppressive Tumor Microenvironment: A Perspective in Ethnopharmacology." *Front. Pharmacol.* 13:886198. doi: 10.3389/fphar. 2022.886198. Retrieved June 21, 2025.

Dorene Petersen, BA, DIP.NT, RH(AHG), is a New Zealand-trained naturopath and expert in herbal medicine, aromatherapy, and holistic wellness with over 48 years of experience. Growing up in New Zealand, she developed a deep love for plants and a lifelong commitment to sharing and supporting wellness through natural remedies and sustainable practices.

In 1978, Dorene founded the American College of Healthcare Sciences (ACHS)—a DEAC-accredited, Certified B Corporation®—dedicated to advancing integrative health education and environmental stewardship. Under her leadership and that of her team, ACHS has become a global pioneer in online education for holistic health, blending evidence-based science with traditional wisdom.

An advocate for accessible and sustainable wellness, Dorene promotes integrating wellness as a daily habit for individuals and organizations alike. Her vision inspired ACHS's corporate and community partnership programs, which help organizations implement meaningful, results-driven wellness initiatives that foster healthier, more resilient workplaces. Dorene has lectured internationally on aromatherapy, medical herbalism, and integrative health. Her work has appeared in publications including *The Herbarist* and the International Herb Association's Herb of the Year books, and she has authored or co-authored over 25 ACHS textbooks. Learn more about Dorene's writing, research, and wellness initiatives at achs.edu.

Curcuma zedoaria, commonly known as zedoary, has a lovely pink bloom and is both culinary and medicinal. *Gail Wood Miller*

Turmeric in Handcrafted Soaps

Marge Powell

For 25 years I owned and operated Magnolia Hill Soap Co., Inc., handcrafting bar and liquid soaps. While I no longer make handcrafted soap for retail consumption, I still manufacture soap for our household use. And even though it is simply for our household there are still guidelines to which I strictly adhere:

1. Use only plant-based coloring
2. Use only essential oil-based scents
3. Use good manufacturing practices

I regularly used turmeric as coloring in my bar soaps. Not only is it attractive, but there are benefits for the skin from the topical use of turmeric. It is said to:

1. Add a natural glow to your skin
2. Treat acne breakouts
3. Slow down skin aging
4. Reduce dark circles
5. Moisturize dry skin
6. Assist with wound healing

Turmeric's topical benefits come from curcumin, a bioactive component with anti-inflammatory and antioxidant properties. Several studies have noted statistically significant improvement in skin disease severity in turmeric/curcumin treatment groups compared with control groups. There were two common themes in the studies I reviewed:

1. Curcumin was demonstrated to have an excellent safety profile in all clinical trials.
2. Further research is required on topical use of turmeric/curcumin, especially relative to effective dosing and application and its effect on hyperpigmentation.

Through the years some of my customers reported back to me that using the soap that contained turmeric was lightening the age spots on their hands. I took this as a bit of imaginative wishful thinking until I did some research on hyperpigmentation. Hyperpigmentation is a common condition that makes some areas of skin darker than others. These spots are sometimes called age spots, sun spots or liver spots and they can occur in just one area of the body or all over.

And perhaps it may be imaginative wishful thinking, or maybe it is not. In perusing the internet on the subject of "Turmeric and hyperpigmentation," I could not find any scientific support for the possibility of turmeric lightening age spots. What I did find was many personal testimonials claiming a turmeric effect on age spots and, of course, myriad products for sale claiming the same. Another topic for solid scientific research.

But given the documented benefits of the topical use of turmeric, it makes sense to include turmeric in the soap you use daily. In bar soap, I have used a heavy concentration of turmeric and used it as a swirl effect or accent in a lighter colored soap. I do not recommend a bar completely colored with turmeric. I made a couple of bars as an experiment. It is not an attractive color (it is very dark, almost black), the lather is orange, and the water that drips from the used soap leaves tan streaks in the soap dish.

But I had not used turmeric in liquid soap, where the holy grail is usually very clear soap. I knew adding turmeric to the liquid soap formula would not result in a clear soap. But I thought the skin benefits outweighed the aesthetic consideration of clear liquid soap. Soap is something that we use daily and spread over our bodies. If that soap also had beneficial aspects, that could be a large gain in our daily hygienic processes. I produced a gallon of liquid soap with the addition of one ounce of powdered turmeric. It resulted in a very dark soap, so I scented it with cinnamon and clove. This is not a scent combination that would work with the general public as many people are sensitive to these essential oils, but it worked for me. I have been using my turmeric liquid soap daily for several weeks now and wait, look, are those my age spots fading? Perhaps, but I have always had a good imagination.

I also produced a gallon of liquid soap with the same formulation minus the turmeric and the formula produces dark soap even without the turmeric. I scented that batch with lavender absolute which turned the batch blue green.

The following are my processes and formulae for the turmeric soap I produced. Note that this assumes the reader has some experience in making soap and it is not intended to be instructional relative to soap making processes.

Turmeric Liquid Soap

Formula
10 ounces KOH (Potassium hydroxide)
19 ounces distilled water
15 ounces coconut oil
15 ounces olive oil
5 ounces wheat germ oil
10 ounces safflower oil
1 ounce organic powdered turmeric
4 ounces of vegetable glycerin
4.5 ounces of essential oil.

I followed a hot process method using a crockpot which produced 4.8 pounds of paste. The first dilution was at a rate of 75% or 3.6 pounds of distilled water. I later added an additional pound of distilled water. When dilution was complete, I added 4 ounces of vegetable glycerin as a sequestering agent and 4.5 ounces of essential oil. This yielded 9.4 pounds of liquid soap or a bit more than a gallon.

The heated oils.   Adding the turmeric to the oils.

The oils and lye begin the hot process.

During the hot process.

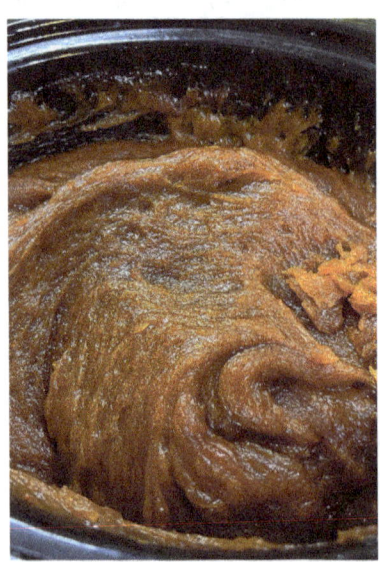

End of the hot process.

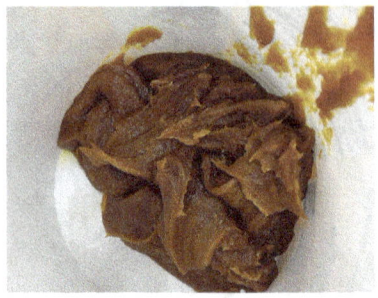

Paste in hydration bucket.

Finished liquid soap.

Turmeric bar soap

I also produced a batch of bar soap using turmeric. The following is the formula and process for the bar soap streaked with turmeric.

20 ounces olive oil
15 ounces coconut oil
12.1 ounces almond oil
10 ounces cocoa butter
10 ounces shea butter
1 ounce organic powdered turmeric

I followed a cold process method. Just before trace (the point at which the mixture thickens and a spoon removed from the mixture will leave a trace on the surface) and after adding the essential oil, I removed approximately 3/4 cup of the soap mixture and added the turmeric, mixing well. I poured my molds with the non-turmeric soap, then introduced the turmeric soap into the mold and mixed slightly with a chopstick. This yielded approximately 18 4-ounce bars of soap.

Turmeric bar soap. *All photos by Marge Powell*

References

Bhattacharya, Sofia. *Skincraft Laboratories.* "7 Benefits of Turmeric for your Skin and How to Use It." https://skincraft.com/blogs/articles/benefits-of-turmeric-for-glowing-skin. Chavan,Priya, Expert reviewer. Accessed 7 April 2025.

Patel, Paras. Wang, Jennifer Y., Mineroff, Jessica, Jagdeo, Jared. *PubMed.* "Evaluation of Curcumin for Dermatologic Conditions: A Systematic Review." https://pubmed.ncbi.nlm.nih.gov/38085369/. Accessed 14 June 2025.

Silver, Natalie. *Healthline.* "Turmeric for Skin: Benefits and Risks." https://www.healthline.com/health/turmeric-for-skin. Donovan, Elizabeth, Editor. Sullivan, Deborah PhD, MSN, RN, CNE, COI, Medical Reviewer. Accessed 14 June 2025.

Vaugh, Alexandra R. Branum, Amy. Sivamani, Raja K. *PubMed.* "Effects of Turmeric (Curcuma longa) on Skin Health: A Systematic Review of the Clinical Evidence." https://pubmed.ncbi.nlm.nih.gov/27213821/. Accessed 14 June 2025.

Marge Powell has been an herbalist for over 45 years and an avid plant person her entire life. Her herbal interests span both the culinary, the medicinal and body care as well as growing herbs. She completed a medicinal herb apprenticeship with Susun Weed and was introduced to herbal body care in workshops conducted by Rosemary Gladstar.

Marge is a passionate cook and most of her cooking is herb-enhanced. She teaches classes in cooking with herbs, bread making, making your own medicines, creating lotions and ointments, making soap, and blending scents. She has conducted hands-on workshops on these and a variety of other herbal topics across the United States. From 2000 until 2024 she owned and operated Magnolia Hill Soap Co., Inc., a producer of herbal soaps and ointments. In 2011 she created Magnolia Hill Nursery which wholesales organic herbs and heirloom vegetables to local garden centers.

She is currently a board member of the International Herb Association (IHA) and the International Herb Association Foundation and is past president of IHA's former Southeastern Region. She has authored numerous herbal articles published in IHA's annual Herb of the Year publications. Recently she has begun collecting data on the history of folk medicine in NE Florida and SE Georgia hoping to shed some light on this often neglected and unstudied aspect of herbal lore.

Bios for Illustrators and Photographers

Susan Belsinger — see bio on page 8

Janice Cox — see bio on page 43

Pat Crocker — see bio on page 95

Matt and Lucie Day — see bio on page 14

Rosemary Roman Davis — see bio on page 52

Karen England — see bio on page 106

Pat Kenny — Pat Kenny, retired medical illustrator, now uses her artistic talent to provide Herb of the Year botanical illustrations. Pat is a long-time member of IHA and HSA and is a supporter of the National Herb Garden in Washington, D.C.

Alicia Mann Alicia Mann, classically trained artist and metalsmith at Heritage Metalworks, LTD, PA, and graduate of Maryland Institute College of Art, combines her love of horticulture with her artistic talents.

Helen Lowe Metzman, MS in Herbal Medicine, Tai Sophis, is a naturalist, gardener, herbalist, and graphic artist. She was director of Jim Duke's Green Farmacy Garden for 6 years. She fondly remembers the time that Jim's white beard was turned "hippie yellow" with turmeric.

Dorene Petersen — see bio on page 227

Marge Powell — see bio on page 234

Douglas Benjamin Reingold, 43-year partner to Pat Kenny, built a 12-plot herb and vegetable garden to support Pat's study and service to the IHA. He sometimes photographs her botanical attempts and herbal antics.

Jane Hawley Stevens — see bio on page 63

Skye Suter — see bio on page 129

Chuck Voigt — see bio on page 132

Tina Marie Wilcox — see bio on page 8

Gail Wood Miller, retired professor of English, is a member of the Musconetcong Watercolor Group and the Garden State Watercolor Society. She now works as a women and children's health and education consultant.

Cover, Illustration, and Photo Credits

Front Cover/Section Covers:
Susan Belsinger

Back Cover:
Left: *Lucie Day*
Center/Right: *Susan Belsinger*

Page Credits:
24, 98: Gail Wood Miller
194: Lucie Day

Pat Kenny and her beautiful turmeric porch plant. *Douglas Reingold*

Celebrating 30 Years of Herb of the Year!

How the Herb of the Year is Selected

Every year since 1995, the International Herb Association has chosen an Herb of the Year™ to highlight. The Horticultural Committee evaluates possible choices based on their being outstanding in at least two of the three major categories: medicinal, culinary, or decorative. Many other herb organizations support the herb of the year selection and we work together to educate the public about these herbs during the year.

Herbs of the Year: Past, Present and Future

1995	Fennel	2013	Elderberry
1996	Monarda	2014	Artemisia
1997	Thyme	2015	Savory
1998	Mint	2016	Capsicum
1999	Lavender	2017	Cilantro & Coriander
2000	Rosemary	2018	Hops
2001	Sage	2019	Agastache
2002	Echinacea	2020	Rubus
2003	Basil	2021	Parsley
2004	Garlic	2022	Viola
2005	Oregano & Marjoram	2023	Ginger
2006	Scented Geraniums	2024	Yarrow
2007	Lemon Balm	2025	Chamomile
2008	Calendula	2026	Turmeric
2009	Bay Laurel	2027	Flax
2010	Dill	2028	Basil & Tulsi
2011	Horseradish	2029	Nasturtium
2012	Rose	2030	Alliums

Books available on www.iherb.org

Join the IHA

Associate with other herb businesses and like-minded folks, network and have fun while you are doing it!

Membership Levels:

$50 Individual Professional
$50 Affiliate Professional
$50 Post Secondary Student

Membership includes:

Membership directory
Herb of the Year™ publication
Quarterly newsletters
Online herbal support
Discounts on conference fees
Promotional support for IHA's Herb of the Year program and
   National Herb Week
Support for National Herb Day
Assocation with a network of diverse herbal businesses

Visit www.iherb.org to see what we are all about!

www.ingramcontent.com/pod-product-compliance
Lightning Source LLC
Chambersburg PA
CBHW070910130626
46555CB00001B/85